help

MY KIDS ARE HURTING

A SURVIVAL GUIDE TO WORKING WITH STUDENTS IN PAIN

MARV PENNER

ZONDERVAN™

GRAND RAPIDS, MICHIGAN 49530 USA

ZONDERVAN.COM/
AUTHOR**TRACKER**

Youth Specialties

www.youthspecialties.com

Youth Specialties

Dedication

This book is dedicated to each of the hurting kids and parents who have trusted me with their stories over the last 35 years.

Thank you for allowing me to see your hearts—even those broken parts you had decided no one would ever see. Thank you for being patient with me when I didn't know what to say or how to help you. Thank you for showing me what it really means to take a risk. Thank you for giving me the sacred privilege of walking with you through dark times—your courage has taught me to trust my heavenly Father more deeply.

Acknowledgements

Putting just one name on the front of a book like this seems so unfair when so many have made an investment. Thanks Jay for letting me write—it's an honor to be associated with the YS/Zondervan family. Urb, your encouragement and eagle eye were so helpful. Kristi, thanks for looking at every word carefully and keeping the grammar police happy with me.

A big thanks to the administration and my colleagues at Briercrest College and Seminary who encourage me in these projects and give me the incredible privilege week after week of standing in a classroom where I'm supposed to be teaching but end up learning new things from my students instead.

Four students who helped me dig for this project deserve a special mention—Megan Jackson, Gabe Choi, Jon Rokochy, and Mike Brownlee—thanks for the research you did. Your help gave me energy on the last lap.

Thanks also to the amazing family God has blessed me with. Tim and Norma, Jeff and Mandy and Melissa—you are such an encouragement when I kick into "writing mode." And Lois...you have so freed me to pursue my dreams—and then you show up in every one of them, supporting, advising, editing, encouraging. Thanks for never letting me do anything alone.

Contents

preface

Choosing to read this book shows that you care about what's going on in the lives of the teenagers you know. As you've spent time with kids, you've probably observed some of the same things I've recently noticed.

- A growing number of adolescents today are hurting deeply—often more deeply than they or many of the adults in their lives are willing to acknowledge.

- Today's kids are faced with issues of increasing complexity, but ignoring these issues is simply not an option. Working with hurting kids should not be taken lightly.

- As youth ministry strategies continue to move toward more decentralized, relational structures (i.e., instead of one expert working with a large group of teenagers, lots of ordinary people work with smaller groups of kids), we're finding that small group leaders, Sunday school teachers, coaches, mentors, and other adult volunteers are playing increasingly significant pastoral roles in students' lives. The paid youth pastor or lead youth worker is, in many cases, one step removed from the nitty-gritty reality of what's going on in the lives of individual students.

- Kids tell their stories to the adults who seem most trustworthy and caring. They don't care if those adults are trained or certified—they just need adults they can count on to listen.

- Youth workers, both volunteer and vocational, often report feeling inadequate and unprepared to respond to the complicated stories kids are telling today. Sadly, some adults may resort to a more relationally distant approach in their work with kids, simply to avoid the possibility of "getting in over their heads."

This book seeks to affirm the significant role you can have as a caring adult involved in the life of a hurting teenager (without getting a degree in clinical psychology). This handy little book will give you some practical help in determining appropriate responses to some of the wild stuff you encounter with kids. It will also introduce you to a number of valuable people-helping skills. Perhaps even more importantly, you'll learn how to recognize your own limitations and study the principles of effective referral—sometimes the wisest course of action will be to involve someone else who is more fully trained or experienced in the diagnosis and treatment of complex adolescent issues.

> "THE THIEF COMES ONLY TO STEAL AND KILL AND DESTROY; I HAVE COME THAT THEY MAY HAVE LIFE, AND HAVE IT TO THE FULL." – JOHN 10:10

Perhaps a disclaimer is in order as we begin. This isn't meant to be a full course in counseling adolescents. This book doesn't cover the complex world of youth culture, the specifics of adolescent development, or critical issues in family systems theory. We won't look in detail at many of the specific challenges kids face. In fact, we may leave out more things than we cover. Think of this book as the equivalent of an intense, relational first-aid course for people who help teenagers. You're not supposed to be a brain surgeon when you finish it, but hopefully you'll know how to stop the bleeding.

So—let's roll up our sleeves and venture into the sometimes messy world of working with hurting teenagers.

Introduction

A casual observer wouldn't have any way of knowing. If someone stopped by and saw the small group of teenagers sitting, chatting, and laughing together in your family room, he might naively assume that the noise and smiles reflect a pretty accurate view of what's going on beneath the surface of each kid's life. Of course, you would know just how wrong he was. You've spent a year getting close to these students, earning their trust, and hearing their stories.

- Tyler's mom and dad are holding their marriage together by a thread, and Tyler is terrified he'll come home one day and find that his dad has moved out.

- Shaina's wearing a long-sleeved T-shirt, as usual, and you really hope it's not because she's cutting her arms again.

- Taryn's coming to terms with a relationship that went bad, so bad it ended in date rape this past summer. But she feels like it's her fault because she'd been drinking and wasn't in a good frame of mind to defend herself.

- Zachary's got that familiar vacant stare in his eyes. You'd love to know what he's thinking, but in all these weeks he's never given you a clue.

- Jasmine hates school because the other girls make fun of her, and this group seems to be the only place she feels safe these days. It's great to see her relaxing for a change.

- Jamal scares you because he's been pretty sporadic in his attendance lately, and you've seen him with some really tough kids at the mall. You're afraid he may be making some bad choices—but at least he's here tonight. Maybe he'll open up a bit and give you a chance to reconnect.

- Lorraine e-mailed you a poem she wrote late one night this week, and it didn't take a rocket scientist to see how hopeless she felt at that moment. Maybe you can get a clue about why when you talk to her later.

- Candace, the pastor's daughter, has told you things that would destroy her mom and dad if they ever found out. She swore you to secrecy, but lately you've been wondering if her parents need to know.

Some days you ask yourself if you'd have volunteered to take on this little Bible study group if you'd had any idea what you were getting into. These kids carry some heavy stuff—and they've trusted you with their stories. I don't have to tell you that you need warmth, empathy, and respect for kids to get them to open up to you. The fact that you're reading this book tells me that the kids you know have decided you're worth trusting.

The problem: Your training amounts to a college psych course and a few things you've learned from watching *Dr. Phil* and *Oprah*. Talk about feeling out of your depth! But the kids don't take your lack of credentials into account. They keep coming back and sharing the secrets of their lives with you. As unqualified as you feel, you haven't got much choice but to listen and help them the best way you know how.

The purpose of this book is to make those moments a little less frightening. It should help answer the question "What do

I do now?" and give you the confidence to listen wisely to what your kids unload on you. I want to remind you again of how important you are in the lives of the students who trust you with their deep hurts.

section one

UNDERSTANDING THE WORLD OF HURTING KIDS

The world of adolescents is a foreign and unfamiliar place for many adults. In this world grown-ups often feel like the aliens—the ones who don't belong. Kids seem to have their own language, fashions, music, and values—and, in fact, they do. But they also have their own fears, struggles, worries, problems, and concerns. And that's where you come in. As an adult who cares about kids, you want to venture into the strange world of teenagers to offer a listening ear, an encouraging word, and a helping hand. As you step into that place, prepare for what you'll find. Your role in the world of teenagers is more important than you'll ever know.

chapter one

FIVE THINGS YOU CAN COUNT ON

1. Kids today are hurting more deeply than they—or we—are willing to admit.

Lots of hurting teenagers have learned to cautiously hide what's really going on inside. They've figured out that opening up to someone—especially an adult—could set them up for more hurt than they're willing to risk. When a kid tries to share his story with someone and is ignored or judged or exposed or given quick advice, for a while he may not make himself that vulnerable again.

When we look at most teenagers, their lives seem so put together. The brand-name wardrobe, cool accessories, and apparently carefree attitudes fool us into thinking everything is fine. But too often, beneath that carefully crafted exterior beats the frightened heart of a little girl or boy who has no one to trust. It's easier for kids to deny what they're feeling and pretend everything is just fine, rather than risk possible rejection by opening up.

Let's think about something even more important: Many of us who work with teenagers find ourselves denying the reality of what's going on with the kids in our care. We pretend everything is okay even when we know the truth. Why the denial? Probably because most of us don't feel equipped to deal with their issues. And besides, getting tangled up in a kid's mess would take more time and energy than we have to give. So we simply carry on the game. As long as nobody's talking about heavy stuff, we don't have to deal with heavy stuff. We try to keep our relationships with our students lighthearted and superficial for fear that if we open the door to deeper issues, we'll have to deal with them.

Many of us haven't even sorted out our own stuff yet, so at all costs we avoid getting involved in someone else's pain. Maybe this explains why some sociologists have described today's teenagers as "the abandoned generation." They don't tell; we don't ask—that way nobody has to worry about what's really going on.

2. The deepest hurt most kids feel is relational.

Neither the chaos of adolescent transitions nor the bizarre circumstances in which kids often find themselves are what wounds kids the most. No, the deepest wounds happen when the people they count on fail to honor that extended trust. When a person who is supposed to provide safety and support walks away and leaves kids on their own, they feel most deeply hurt. We are talking about abandonment—relational, emotional, and at times even physical abandonment. This generation has been left to care for itself. Unfortunately, the deepest betrayal of trust kids experience is often family based. And even more upsetting, in too many cases a kid loses his relationship with his dad. Kids need people in their lives whom they can count on—no matter what. In the absence of trustworthy people, they're often left to do whatever they must in order to survive. That can lead to all kinds of destructive and dangerous choices.

3. Kids will decide whom they'll trust with their deepest pain.

Most teenagers have little or no access to nonparental adults, particularly ones who know them well enough to help teenagers navigate the realities of their complicated adolescent world. Formal systems to deal with kids at risk have been established in many communities. Guidance counselors in schools, child protection officers and social workers, walk-in medical clinics, toll-free crisis lines, after-school programs, and counseling centers invite hurting kids to tell their stories. But when an adolescent really hurts, he longs for a relationship with someone who cares about him on a personal level—someone who knows his name and is available outside of office hours. Kids share their lives with people who've taken the time to prove their trustworthiness. They don't care about the education, certification, or experience of the people they choose to trust. They just need to know those people care.

4. The church has a long way to go.

The idea of true community deeply appeals to teenagers. After all, they're in the process of disconnecting from their families and developing social identities of their own. If our churches functioned the way they were originally intended to, they could provide places of shelter and safety for hurting teenagers. The community of faith has at its disposal unique resources intended to bring hope and help to hurting people of all ages. Unfortunately, for the most part those resources remain unacknowledged and untapped. Many churches have lost their ability to provide a welcome for hurting people—especially adolescents, who often represent an even greater challenge because of the generational misunderstanding that plagues them. The fact that you're reading this book tells me you want to provide hurting kids with a way to experience love, acceptance, and hope. When our churches become the communities they're meant to be, we'll see hurting people of all ages finding help.

5. The stakes are high.

At the risk of setting off alarm bells, we need to face a sad and frightening reality: The number of adults that kids are willing to trust may be quite small. It takes time to build the kinds of relationships that encourage them to open up. Not many adults are willing to make this kind of investment. If a teenager has trusted you enough to tell you her story, she has given you a sacred gift. You may be the only adult in a position to help her make wise choices. I don't want to be melodramatic about this, but if we choose to ignore a student who trusts us enough to tell us her story, she may have no choice but to bury her feelings and try to cope on her own.

chapter two

EIGHT UNIQUE CHALLENGES OF WORKING WITH KIDS IN PAIN

When we spend time with hurting kids, we quickly realize that working with teenagers differs in many ways from working with other age groups. Teenagers are often dealing with adult issues but without the emotional resources and relational maturity to do so wisely. Think with me about some of the unique issues we face when we work with at-risk adolescents.

1. THE OFTEN INTENSE URGENCY OF IT

Helping hurting kids can involve the frightening reality of working with people engaged in immediately dangerous and destructive behavior. Adolescents believe they're invincible—"Nothing will happen to me." They may be participating in high-risk activities without recognizing the dangers involved. Promiscuity, substance abuse, violence, eating disorders, and self-injurious behaviors are all part of the adolescent landscape. Yet our kids may be oblivious to the risks of getting involved in these activities. It means we can't stand idly by. The potential for long-term damage is just too great.

2. THE SOMETIMES ARMS-LENGTH NATURE OF IT

This may involve third-person helping because kids typically confide in each other first. "I think my friend is considering suicide. What should I say?" "My friend has a drinking problem. Can I do anything?" "My friend thinks she might be pregnant. Who should she call?" We find ourselves called upon to provide support and counsel for kids we may never meet. The teenager who needs the help either doesn't know or doesn't trust us, so he talks to a friend whom he does know and trust. We feel a bizarre combination of responsibility and helplessness because we know what's at stake but have no way of dealing with the problem directly. It means we have no choice but to trust the kid who asks for our help and to encourage him to stay involved in the life of his hurting friend.

3. THE FRUSTRATING ONE-SIDEDNESS OF IT

We rarely get the whole story—not because kids are trying to withhold the truth, but because they simply can't be objective. Their stories are always tangled up in several others. They share their personal perspectives on situations, but we know these versions may be inaccurate or incomplete. Teenagers will share wild accounts of abusive, unreasonable parents who may turn out to be the most loving, caring parents you've ever met. You'll hear about teachers who obviously don't get it, classmates who are complete jerks, and friends who are just plain mean. The problem is we have no way of knowing what is true and what isn't. The bottom line: For a teenager in pain, perception is reality. It means we need to take what we hear with an appropriate dose of caution. We must be careful not to jump to conclusions until we've heard the whole story, while still offering the adolescent the respect of listening without judgment. It's a balancing act.

> TELL PARENTS YOU WON'T BELIEVE EVERYTHING THEIR KIDS SAY ABOUT THEM IF THEY PROMISE NOT TO BELIEVE EVERYTHING THEIR KIDS SAY ABOUT YOU.

4. THE MADDENING UPS AND DOWNS OF IT

Kids sometimes seem developmentally schizophrenic—slipping back and forth between adult thinking and childlike immaturity in a way that seems almost random at times. It can be frustrating to observe them processing circumstances with wisdom and maturity during one conversation, only to see them deteriorate into naive helplessness the next time they need to talk. It can feel like three steps forward and two steps back. We must realize that adolescents do, in fact, straddle the worlds of children and adults. Sometimes kids are just too scared to deal with pain as adults would. We honor hurting kids when we give them permission to move back and forth between these two worlds—respecting and validating them as young adults but also protecting them as vulnerable children. Most teenagers have very few adults in their lives who understand that this critical tension is one of their survival mechanisms.

5. THE COMMUNITY CONNECTEDNESS OF IT

Working with hurting kids often requires us to cooperate with established community agencies such as the police department, probation officers, social workers, hospitals, schools, and so on. These systems were put in place to deal with many of the issues hurting teenagers face. Unfortunately, they're an unfamiliar world for a lot of people who work in the church. We often treat these secular helpers with disdain and distrust, and sadly, they often have the same cynicism about people in the church. It's time for us to learn to work together. We can't afford to alienate ourselves from these valuable resources. Frankly, in most cases we have no choice. If established agencies are in place to deal with specific issues (such as abuse, divorce, mental illness, and suicide intervention), then they are well positioned to help and, in fact, may be legally required to get involved. Certainly the bureaucratic machinery can be frustrating at times, but make no mistake—it's wise for us to build bridges of cooperation for the sake of the students we work with and for the sake of the gospel.

6. THE PERSONAL RISKS OF IT

Be ready to experience some emotional intensity and maybe some verbal abuse if you decide to get involved with hurting kids. They may have some very deep feelings connected to painful relationships from their pasts. As an adult involved in kids' lives, you might unknowingly represent something or someone that hurt them in the past. I happen to be a "dad-aged" man, so kids transfer to me a lot of the disappointment and anger they feel in their "dad memories." (The technical term for this is *transference*.) This generational reaction may mean that we'll have to endure seemingly random outbursts, anger, and lack of regard from the very kids we're trying to help—despite the fact that they *invited* us into their stories. By the way, teenagers often feel most free to vent their anger on the people they trust most deeply. As part of our ministry to these kids, we can offer them safe relationships where some of this passion can surface and then be redirected toward more positive ends.

7. THE SOMETIMES APPARENT HOPELESSNESS OF IT

Sending hurting kids back into the relational mess that produced their pain in the first place can create a sense of hopelessness in our efforts. The terrified victim of bullying who heads right back to school where she's an easy target; the kid whose dad has called him stupid for the last 14 years goes straight home after you've spent an hour telling him he's all right; the gang member who's trying to kick his drug habit has to return to the horrible neighborhood where his addiction started. Just when we feel like we're making some headway with kids, we realize how fragile that growth can be. It's maddening when we realize the context that created the problem (often the family) is thoroughly damaging and isn't likely to change. One of the greatest challenges we face is helping kids understand that they can be healthy, even when unhealthy people surround them.

8. THE OFTEN INVISIBLE RESULTS OF IT

This can feel like thankless work. In many cases the outcome and results of our investment in a hurting teenager may not be visible for many years to come. In fact, we may not hear the end of the story until heaven. Because adolescents are in the midst of multiple transitions—physiologically, emotionally, spiritually, socially, morally, cognitively—progress can be difficult to gauge. Kids may not remember the things we say until months or even years later. Because they may not be ready to make the right choices in the immediate reality of their circumstances, they may not implement our wisdom until they're older. Working with kids is like walking a short portion of a long journey with someone. We must understand the value of our presence in light of the big picture. Those who need immediate affirmation for their ministry work probably will be frustrated by working with hurting teenagers. The payoff may happen years down the road. We may not be there to see the results of our involvement. In fact, someone else may get the credit for changes we helped bring about, which is humbling. Get used to it if you choose to work with wounded kids.

SO WHY WOULD ANYONE IN THEIR RIGHT MIND WANT TO WORK WITH HURTING KIDS?

When I talk with people who are regularly involved with hurting kids, I often ask them why they do it. Given the risks and personal costs involved, I'm amazed at the consistent responses I receive—four answers over and over. Perhaps you would also echo one of these reasons:

> **"Somebody did it for me."** You remember being a hurting teenager with nowhere to turn, but a caring adult took the time to hear your story and give you the support and help you needed. You know how much it meant in your life, and now you simply want to offer a hurting kid what you received when you were her age. In a very appropriate way, it feels like you're giving something back—and you are.

"Nobody did it for me." As a teenager you faced your pain alone. You reached out to adults whom you hoped could help you but never found one willing to step into the gap. You know the lonely memories of floundering through the chaos of adolescence. Now you want to make sure no teenager misses out the way you did. You can sense when kids suffer deep pain—just by looking at them. This awareness motivates you to be there for them.

"It's the call of God on my life." You're naturally drawn to hurting teenagers. You can't help it. You don't find struggling students burdensome. In fact, you seem to have a sixth sense that helps you sniff out kids who need help. Rapport with them comes easily, and you don't understand why other people seem so terrified of kids who need help. Recognize this as a gift and use it faithfully. You're part of a small minority set apart by God for a special ministry. Don't take it for granted.

"I've seen it work." Even though the odds seem to be against you, you're incredibly excited to see a changed life. You've known the thrill of having God work through you before, and you're willing to put yourself in that place again. With each story you hear, you learn to trust God more deeply.

Whatever our reasons for helping hurting students, we're amazed God chooses to use us in the lives of kids. There is no greater joy for those who experience it.

section two

BECOMING A PERSON WHO CAN HELP HURTING KIDS

"FROM THE LEAST TO THE GREATEST, ALL ARE GREEDY FOR GAIN; PROPHETS AND PRIESTS ALIKE, ALL PRACTICE DECEIT. THEY DRESS THE WOUND OF MY PEOPLE AS THOUGH IT WERE NOT SERIOUS. 'PEACE, PEACE,' THEY SAY, WHEN THERE IS NO PEACE." —JEREMIAH 6:13-14

Not just anyone can make a difference in the life of a hurting teenager. While some may possess more natural gifts for this kind of work than others, it's not a requirement of the job. And if we spend time with students, let them get to know us, show them respect, and listen to what they have to say, they'll start to reveal their secret lives to us. This is where helping teenagers can get scary—if we're unprepared. Fear, busyness, selfishness, and dishonesty can keep us from taking kids' hurts seriously. Like the prophets of Jeremiah's day, we can either gloss over the pain kids share with us and pretend it's no big deal, or we can do everything in our power to become the kind of people willing to go deeper with kids and help them find hope and healing in the midst of their confusion and pain.

chapter three

WHAT DO HURTING KIDS WANT FROM US?

Maybe like young Frodo in *The Lord of the Rings* you're wondering why you've been chosen for this formidable task of working with kids who hurt. You feel as if others could do a much better job. Don't assume students will take their problems to the best educated or most experienced adults they know. Trustworthiness and respect are much higher priorities for most kids. This puts frontline youth workers—often volunteers—in the best position to know the hearts of their students.

Teenagers appear to look for three things when they decide whom to trust. This "triple A" relationship helps us connect most deeply with hurting kids.

- Availability: Teenagers look for someone who's accessible, not too busy to take the time to get to know them and hear their stories. But availability isn't just about making time on our calendars. It's also about having a welcoming spirit—about making room in our hearts. Availability says we have time and emotional space to share life—even when it gets messy. It tells kids they're not a bother. It doesn't take long for kids to decide you're not available when you've got more kids in your group than you can handle. Keep the ratio of adults to students small if you want kids to see you as being available.

- Authenticity: Kids need to know adults who are real—their walks match their talk. This generation of adolescents is wary—and weary—of the hypocrisy they've seen in older generations. They respect adults who say with their lives, "What you see is what you get."

They seem attracted to people who are willing to live transparent and honest lives. The last thing they need is perfection—in fact, not much will alienate kids more quickly than an adult who presents a flawless exterior. It's intimidating—and besides, they're too smart to believe it anyway.

- Acceptance: Lots of teenagers feel misunderstood, diminished, and disrespected by the people around them. Parents often impose expectations and demands that make kids feel as if they can never measure up. They are constantly feeling judged—and often found wanting. An adult who enjoys kids without critique is a welcome exception to what many of them experience on a regular basis. They long for people to value them for who they are instead of what they do. A relationship of nonjudgmental acceptance opens the door to trust and deep sharing. This doesn't mean we overlook areas in their lives that need to be challenged—but it does mean kids know they're safe with us.

chapter four
WHAT ABOUT BOUNDARIES?

If only helping were as easy as being available, authentic, and accepting! The problem is that offering this kind of help without limits and discernment can actually destroy our relationships with kids—not to mention other important areas in our lives that are vulnerable to abuse. Think about it for a minute. What happens when we make ourselves available to kids 24/7/365? What happens when we tell all and don't guard certain areas of our lives from the scrutiny of impressionable teenagers? And perhaps most importantly, what happens when we accept everything about a kid without challenging her to grow and change? Let's take a closer look.

THE DANGERS OF UNRESTRICTED AVAILABILITY

We can easily see the loneliness of kids today and find ourselves vowing not to be another adult who abandons and disappoints them. But as some of us have learned the hard way, kids will take all we give them. I've seen too many well-meaning youth workers tell groups of kids, "Call me anytime" or "I'm here for you whenever you need me"—and then gradually develop a growing resentment toward students who take them up on their offers.

If we provide our students with unlimited access, our primary relationships begin to suffer. This includes our spouses, our own children, and our adult friends. When those important relationships begin to take second place, we quickly become unbalanced and lose our effectiveness with kids. Now our time with students begins to feel like an intrusion, and we find ourselves locking our doors, turning off our cell phones, and turning out the lights for fear of an invasion.

Availability is as much about attitude as the number of hours we offer our students. Teenagers look for adults who enjoy being with them and are willing to make some extra time to ensure that happens. They understand that no one is actually accessible 24/7, so they really appreciate knowing how and when they can get in touch with us.

By the way, on some rare occasions you may legitimately say to a kid in a specific time of need, "Over these next couple of days feel free to call me anytime." If you know he's in the midst of a crisis at home or something big is happening in his life, let him know you're opening up your window of availability. Most kids will respect your need to "have a life" and won't take inappropriate advantage of your generosity.

HERE'S A HINT
LET KIDS KNOW WHEN YOU *ARE AVAILABLE* RATHER THAN TELLING THEM WHEN YOU'RE NOT. SOMETHING LIKE, "I'LL TRY TO BE ONLINE FOR AN HOUR OR TWO EVERY MONDAY NIGHT AROUND EIGHT O'CLOCK" OR "FEEL FREE TO DROP BY THE HOUSE ANYTIME ON SATURDAY MORNINGS" IS MORE HELPFUL THAN JUST SAYING, "DON'T CALL ME DURING MEALTIMES OR ON WEEKENDS."

THE DANGERS OF UNCENSORED AUTHENTICITY

Authenticity does not mean we uninhibitedly open every corner of our lives to all of our students. We're the grown-ups—they're the kids. The issue is honesty. Are you pretending to be someone you're not? That's hypocrisy! Are you choosing not to share every doubt or struggle? That's wisdom.

Perhaps you find yourself hiding behind a facade that you believe your kids will accept more easily than the "real you." Authenticity begins when we decide to be honest with ourselves and with God. When the psalmist says, "Search me, O God…test me…see if there is any offensive way in me" (Psalm 139:23, 24), the risk of honesty with God and self becomes apparent. Authenticity is all about who we are and how we live our lives. Teenagers need to know that adults don't have all their theological and personal ducks in a row, either. Students gain hope when they see an adult who is honestly wrestling with the struggles of life in a broken world.

So what does that kind of authenticity look like? It's important to understand the concept of *ministry-motivated* transparency. The idea is that we allow kids into our lives to the extent that our relational risk represents a growth opportunity for them. The contrast, a let-it-all-hang-out approach—what I call "emotional exhibitionism"—is all about our need to vent or, even more selfishly, our need for teenagers to affirm and need us.

The bottom line: There are many things kids shouldn't have to worry about. Some of the teenagers we work with already know far more about their parents' dysfunctional lives than they want to know. They don't need another adult baring it all to them. When kids see we're willing to open up to them appropriately, they will trust our authenticity and pursue the same thing in their relationships.

Perhaps having adult accountability partners our own age and gender would be a more appropriate means of addressing and processing our personal issues. Honest self-evaluation is the first step toward personal health and wholeness. In the process we may become aware of significant areas of spiritual doubt or behavioral issues that would disqualify us from ministry if exposed. What do we do about that? There's no shame in taking a break from working with kids to work on our own lives for a time. If the foundation of your faith isn't solid, and if you're not intentional about pursuing a lifestyle beyond reproach, consider reviewing David's prayer in its entirety ("Search me, O God" from Psalm 139)—and see what God exposes in you. We can't take our students where we're not willing to go ourselves.

HERE'S A HINT
FILTER YOUR LEVEL OF PERSONAL DISCLOSURE THROUGH
THE LAW OF LOVE IN EPHESIANS 4:29, WHICH REMINDS US,
"DO NOT LET ANY UNWHOLESOME TALK COME OUT OF YOUR
MOUTHS, BUT ONLY WHAT IS HELPFUL FOR BUILDING OTHERS
UP ACCORDING TO THEIR NEEDS, THAT IT MAY BENEFIT
THOSE WHO LISTEN." ASK YOURSELF, *IS THIS CONVERSATION
HELPING MY STUDENT FRIEND OR IS IT JUST SOMETHING I
NEED TO GET OFF MY CHEST? WILL THIS BUILD UP OR TEAR
DOWN THE KID WHO HEARS IT?*

THE DANGERS OF UNLIMITED ACCEPTANCE

Let's be honest: Kids do some things that are simply unacceptable. But while certain behaviors, relationships, language,
attitudes, and choices need to be challenged, they don't make
the kid unacceptable. Love without boundaries leaves kids
feeling uneasy and afraid, while boundaries without love can
make them feel like failures who will never measure up.

But it gets trickier when adults who don't have relationships with these students are still reprimanding them; students feel judged and misunderstood. They've got plenty of
those kinds of adults in their lives—teachers, bosses, cops—
and maybe even their parents. Our challenge is to establish
the kind of relationships with our students that will gives us
the right to call them on areas where they're out of line.

After telling us about things they've done—things they
know are unacceptable—our students constantly ask if we'll
still love them. This is especially true when they choose to
share secrets they've kept hidden from others. When kids
decide to let someone know what's really going on under the
surface, you may hear some pretty ugly stories. Responses of
shock, horror, disgust, and quick judgment won't help at this
point. In most cases kids will already know they've blown it.

They don't need their failures reinforced. Yet it's important for us to let them know that we believe in living by standards.

An important heads-up: Be sensitive to the fact that kids who are victims of others' choices will often accept the blame for what happened to them. "If only I hadn't been so stupid, I wouldn't have been raped that night." "If I was a better kid, maybe my dad wouldn't drink all the time." Ask God to give you the discernment to help them differentiate between victimization and the natural consequences of their choices.

One of the adolescent's key tasks is to establish a personal set of beliefs and values that will become the basis for living as an adult. Because teenagers are in the process of disengaging from family and their parents' values, they're often left with only their friends to guide them. You've seen their friends! Does that give you a sense of how important it is to make sure you have the necessary level of trust and involvement with your students so you can help them in their quest for personal morality?

HERE'S A HINT
DON'T FORGET THAT BECAUSE OF THE RELATIONSHIP OF TRUST A STUDENT HAS OFFERED YOU, YOU MAY BE ONE OF THE FEW ADULTS IN HER LIFE WHO HAS THE FREEDOM TO CHALLENGE HER IN AREAS OF INAPPROPRIATE BEHAVIOR, DESTRUCTIVE RELATIONSHIPS, OR TOXIC ATTITUDES. THINK ABOUT YOUR RESPONSIBILITY TO CARE SO DEEPLY THAT YOU WON'T LET HER GET AWAY WITH THINGS THAT WILL HURT HER IN THE LONG RUN.

chapter five

WHAT'S YOUR STYLE—HUGGER, TEACHER, PREACHER, OR SURGEON?

Each of us handles working with hurting kids from a unique perspective. Some of us are tough, and some are gentle. Some act like parents, others more like friends. Some of us are great listeners while some are more likely to tell kids what to do next. Some of us are intuitive and can easily see what's going on at the heart of a kid's life; others need a lot of tangible evidence to figure out what's really happening. There's no one "right" way, but a number of factors play a part in determining our individual helping styles. Our temperament, background, theology, and relational baggage all contribute to the formation of our own personal approach to helping kids through tough times.

It's valuable for us to identify our own default approaches to helping kids, as each style has its own strengths and weaknesses. When we're aware of the benefits and challenges of each method, we can make sure that kids are receiving the best possible help. This happens when we're able to balance our approach or when we invite someone who possesses the strengths we lack to join us in the relationship.

VICTIMS OR CHOOSERS?

Two factors seem especially important in determining how we will seek to help kids who share their stories with us. The first factor deals with how much responsibility we place on the kids for their current circumstances. Are kids messed up because they've made bad choices and now must live with the natural consequences? Or are they messed up because awful things have happened to them outside of their control?

The vertical line in the diagram below illustrates this.

I GENERALLY THINK KIDS HAVE PROBLEMS
BECAUSE OF BAD CHOICES THEY MAKE.

$\updownarrow$

I GENERALLY THINK KIDS HAVE PROBLEMS
BECAUSE BAD THINGS HAPPEN TO THEM.

People at the top of the line would say that kids are account-able for creating their own messes, and therefore, they should take responsibility for their own choices. If you take this position, you believe that kids are choosing individuals who need to learn to take full responsibility for their choices. When you choose bad friends, you increase your chances of getting into trouble. When you start using drugs, you're more likely to become addicted. When you're driven to be thin, you set yourself up for an eating disorder. When you date that loser, chances are good you'll get hurt.

The bottom of the arrow says that kids get into trouble because of the awful circumstances in their lives. They grew up in a bad neighborhood, so they couldn't help getting caught up in all the bad things that happened around them. Their parents were too busy to spend time with them, so they developed inappropriate ways to get attention from others. They were sexually abused as children, so they're deeply wounded and don't know how to enjoy healthy relation-ships. They're bullied in school or have a learning disability or an alcoholic parent—you get the idea.

Some of us tend to see kids primarily as helpless victims while others see them as choosers or responsible for their own circumstances.

RELATIONALLY INTIMATE OR DETACHED?

The other variable that shapes our responses to kids is more personality based and relates to how open and involved we are in our own relationships. Do we find it easy to get close to kids, or do we tend to stay at arm's length? You'll see this contrasted on the continuum below.

I TEND TO STAY MORE AT ARM'S LENGTH IN MY RELATIONSHIPS WITH THE KIDS I WORK WITH.	←——————→	I TEND TO DEEPLY CONNECT WITH AND QUITE EASILY GET CLOSE TO THE KIDS I WORK WITH.

Those who tend toward the left end of the spectrum believe staying somewhat relationally detached from hurting kids is valuable. It's not that they don't care. In fact, they would say it's just the opposite. They recognize the value of retaining some objectivity in their handling of problems. They believe that if they get too tangled up in the details of the stories, they may not be able to offer the kind of help students need.

People who live at the right side of the spectrum love getting close to kids. They're vulnerable and transparent with the kids they know. The kids' stories emotionally impact these adults. They often share parts of their own stories to let kids know they understand what's being said. They believe kids need to have at least one adult who knows them deeply and is willing to show that love by being open with them.

COMPARISON OF THE FOUR STYLES

So what happens when we put the two diagrams together? Notice the interesting combinations that emerge. Chances are you'll be able to relate to at least one of these patterns as you offer help to hurting kids.

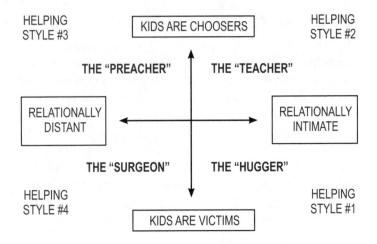

	KIDS ARE CHOOSERS	
HELPING STYLE #3		HELPING STYLE #2
THE "PREACHER"		THE "TEACHER"
RELATIONALLY DISTANT	← →	RELATIONALLY INTIMATE
THE "SURGEON"		THE "HUGGER"
HELPING STYLE #4		HELPING STYLE #1
	KIDS ARE VICTIMS	

Helping Style #1—The Hugger

You're probably a hugger if you tend to see the world as a tough place for kids to grow up—an environment that makes kids vulnerable to all sorts of abuses by the media, by adults, and even by the church. You generally see kids as victims and you like to connect closely with those who need your help. It's not hard to see why I call you a "hugger." Hurting kids want your comfort and encouragement. Their pain comes as a result of awful things that have happened to them.

The hugger wants to make sure kids won't be hurt again. Huggers are "there for" the kids who need them—they're emotionally connected and relationally available. They offer their consistent presence as a lifeline to wounded teenagers. "Count on me," they say. "I won't abandon you. Call me if you need me." Huggers offer their presence in a nonjudgmental way. While not blind to the fact that the behaviors and attitudes of the kids they work with need to be changed, they believe the best way for that to happen is to act as sounding boards and advocates. Huggers have often lived with their own pain in a cruel world and feel comfortable sharing their stories with kids to let them know that others have experienced similar hurts.

Helping Style #2—The Teacher

If you find yourself looking at the self-made disasters in a kid's life and asking, "What were you thinking?" then your helping style is probably that of a teacher. You enjoy getting close to kids, but you shake your head in disbelief at some of the dumb choices they make. If these kids just had a little guidance—someone to give them some advice along the way—maybe they'd wise up and save themselves some grief.

"Teachers" want to help kids learn from the mistakes they've made. They're great at helping kids reframe events and understand them from new points of view. They realize that teenagers will have lots more opportunities to make bad choices, but teachers believe that some new skills and a bit of accountability might save kids from a lifetime of heartache. Destructive behaviors must be unlearned and replaced with healthy ones. Teachers love to give practical advice to kids who are open to changing. For teachers, helping is about reminding kids that their choices really do make a difference.

Helping Style #3—The Preacher

You know a heart of rebellion beats in every one of us, and that includes the kids you work with. The evidence is so clear. Their lives are marked by promiscuity, anger, substance abuse, gossip, and self-injury, to name just a few—all clear violations of God's standards. The "preacher" in you just wants these kids to see that they're headed in the wrong direction. You know that the path they're on leads to more pain, and you're passionate about calling them to renounce their negative behaviors and start changing their lifestyles.

Preachers often can't understand why kids are so stubborn and unrepentant. Confession of sin and godly obedience are such obvious solutions to the choices being made. Duh! The preacher wants kids to see that the sins being expressed through their behaviors and relationships clearly violate God's standards. It simply comes down to making a decision: Live your own way and keep messing up, or live God's way and experience what you were created for. Most preachers see themselves as rescuing kids from traps that have them hopelessly bound. They care deeply about kids and just want to see them set free. The passion that drives preachers can be quite intense.

Helping Style #4—The Surgeon

If you're a surgeon, nothing is simple or obvious. You look at a hurting kid's heart the way a doctor looks at an X-ray. Deep, hidden issues must be understood to determine what the real problem is. Sure, some things are apparent on the outside, but to understand what's really going on, you know you need to look under the surface. So many factors shape a teenager's attitudes, behaviors, and emotions—family of origin, temperament, abuses, genetics, relationships, friendships, education—the list could go on and on. When you look at hurting kids, they often seem like bit players in a complex mystery movie. Your job is to unravel the plot.

People helpers who take a surgical approach are concerned with the deeper, hidden problems that feed the more visible symptoms in kids' lives. Like detectives, they keep a safe relational distance from kids so as to maintain their objectivity. "Surgeons" tend to see kids as victims of their environments, their genetics, their parents, or their pasts. They believe that behind every dysfunctional behavior and destructive relational pattern lie deeply rooted, underlying issues that need to be exposed and eliminated. The surgeon sees the subconscious as the driving force for much of what kids experience. These deeply buried issues need to be brought to the surface so they can be dealt with. This means exploring the family of origin, exposing distorted self-esteem, challenging inaccurate assumptions that kids have made about who they are, and connecting destructive behaviors with the motivations that drive them.

THE HAZARDS OF IMBALANCE OR ONE-DIMENSIONAL APPROACHES IN EACH HELPING STYLE

Limitations of Huggers

The hugger—

- is all about keeping it warm and fuzzy.

- tends not to hold teenagers responsible for the choices they've made—often providing very little accountability, just lots of encouragement and comfort.

- may not provide kids with any reason to move out of "victim mode"—in fact they may reinforce it because of the emotional fulfillment it provides for the hugger (often referred to as "enabling" unhealthy patterns).

- is easily sucked in by kids who are used to emotionally controlling or manipulating adults.

- can feel inappropriately responsible for kids' emotional well-being.

- communicates only the mercy and kindness of God and downplays his holiness and justice.

Limitations of Teachers

The teacher—

- is all about being the expert—always has advice.

- can feel very "top-down" to a hurting kid.

- may ignore the pain and woundedness of the student seeking help.

- often switches to advice-giving mode before taking the time to hear the whole story.

- focuses on the future and ignores past and present realities.

- emphasizes behavior modification as a means of pain management—but it may not be that simple.

Limitations of Preachers

The preacher—

- is all about holding kids accountable for the choices they've made.

- tends to lack empathy and understanding; can cause a kid to feel as if the preacher is pointing a finger of accusation and condemnation.

- requires no relational connection, empathy, or mutual trust—can seem very condescending to a hurting teenager.

- is usually a better talker than listener.

- may leave a kid feeling as if the whole thing is his fault, which may reinforce an already shameful sense of responsibility.

- often focuses on the wrath and judgment of God and ignores his mercy and kindness.

Limitations of Surgeons

The surgeon—

- is all about being a psychological detective.

- tends to make kids feel as if they're specimens to be scientifically examined or dissected.

- has no relational feeling when helping—can be cold, calculating, and clinical.

- focuses on the problem and often has very little to say about appropriate solutions.

- reinforces the notion that the kid has no responsibility—after all, the problem lies mysteriously in his wounded subconscious.

- can create a justification for blaming others: "It's not my fault—you can't hold me responsible for something I'm not even aware of."

THE BEST APPROACH

"So what's the right way?" you ask. Each situation is so unique. Obviously, sometimes a kid needs a preacher more than a hugger. Some students' complex stories require a careful surgeon to uncover and diagnose the deep issues driving bizarre behaviors and random emotions. And sometimes a gentle teacher who can nudge a hurting kid in a new direction is all that's needed to get things on track again. Each helping style is valid and necessary in the ministry we offer to hurting adolescents. However, we must realize that we may not be able to be all things to all kids.

Some good news: As I look at the descriptions of these helping styles outlined above, I can't help but see a biblical picture of God's character expressed in each of the terms. He is the "hugger" described as the Comforter in Jeremiah 8, the God of compassion and comfort we find in 2 Corinthians 1, the high priest who understands our pain in Hebrews 4. He is the teacher Jesus promises in John 14 and the guide to truth the psalmist appeals to in Psalm 25. He is the preacher who convicts us of sin as described in John 16, and who calls us to holy choices in 1 Peter 1 and to costly obedience in 1 John 2. He is the surgeon who searches and knows our inmost being as the psalmist invites in Psalm 139, who explores deep and hidden things as described in Daniel 2 and as we read in Hebrews 4:13, "Nothing in all creation is hidden from God's sight. Everything is uncovered and laid bare before the eyes of him to whom we must give account."

God is actually all four of the helpers we've defined—a gentle hugger, a wise teacher, a powerful preacher, and an insightful surgeon. He offers hope and healing in a perfectly balanced way. This can give you a great deal of confidence as you examine your own imbalances.

God can always use us as part of the larger plan he has for these kids he cares for so much. He compensates for our personal ministry lopsidedness in several ways. For instance, when needed, he gives us the wisdom and ability to operate outside our default method of relating to kids. I'm sure you've had times when you've been talking with a student and found yourself saying things that were quite out of character and beyond your own wisdom. But those words turned out to be just what she needed to hear. God was speaking through you in the way he knew would best serve her needs. Because God dwells in us by his Spirit, he enables us to speak in his voice to those who need to hear from him. It's quite a privilege and certainly a significant responsibility. Of course, this approach requires sensitivity to God's presence and a willingness to obey when he asks us to speak in voices that aren't natural for us.

Another way God accommodates our ministry inadequacies is to use more than one person to speak truth into the life of a student. I'm a hugger, so I often find myself surrounded by kids who need encouragement and protection. It's something I do quite well, but I recognize that at some point in their healing journey, they may need a teacher or preacher to help them take responsibility and to make good choices in the future. Or maybe a surgeon could help them decipher subconscious issues from their pasts. If I hold my relationships with hurting students in an open hand, I find that God will often use a number of different people to help kids on their way to healing and wholeness. This will mean being part of a team where each person knows her gifts and contributions and is willing to share the ministry with others.

There's no room for adults who are jealous or leaders who hoard their relationships with students—not if we want to see God bring complete healing into the lives of hurting kids. Take a moment to think about your ministry team. Who are the huggers, the teachers, the preachers, and the surgeons? Remember—each one has a part to play, and we must celebrate the diversity we see around us.

chapter six

SORTING THROUGH YOUR OWN BAGGAGE

One final thought before we leave this discussion of becoming a person God can use to bring healing to kids. Our own stories play a huge role in shaping our responses to hurting kids. Each person's path has been unique. Some of us can't identify at all with the deep pain of the teenagers we meet. Our own adolescence may have been relatively pain-free (or marked by denial), so we find it hard to respond with empathy to a wounded student. Others experienced a deep world of hurt as teenagers, and the stories we hear from kids sadly reflect our own tales of woe. We relate to their hurt at a profound level—often reexperiencing the pain of events that may have happened to us years ago. Whether your story is one of joy or hurt, you need to recognize how your past expresses itself in the help you offer.

If your childhood and adolescent life was generally safe and pleasant, you may find yourself feeling impatient with hurting kids. Why can't they just get their act together? you wonder. They may be clamoring for attention, exaggerating their stories, or wallowing in their victimization. The solutions to their problems will seem obvious to you, and you may find it difficult to give them time to unravel the tangled emotions they're feeling. Remember: You're hearing their stories from the point of view of an adult who never went through these things. Too easily we forget how traumatic and emotionally consuming the transitions of adolescence are for most teenagers. We forget how lonely kids can be.

If you find you need more patience with struggling kids, ask God to give you eyes to see what's really going on. Avoid the temptation to give quick advice and learn from the courageous honesty of kids who are willing to face their pain directly. You may even find some value in reviewing portions of your own adolescent story to see if you have some unfinished business that is affecting your life today. Working with kids can evoke or reawaken our own issues, and that's not always a bad thing.

Another possibility is that your adolescence was difficult and stressful. Spending time with teenagers in pain feels like a crazy déjà vu. The memories of your own hurts flood back quickly, and you want to be there for kids who are going through the same things you experienced at their age. You empathize deeply with the brokenness of kids who've been abused or betrayed by people they should be able to trust. You easily connect with these hurting kids because you understand their pain.

Don't mistakenly assume you'll automatically be able to help kids just because you can relate to their pain. Sometimes our logic is, "Because my dad was an alcoholic, I can help other children of alcoholics" or "Because I was sexually abused as a child, I will be a big help to other survivors of abuse." Unfortunately, helping someone work through his pain is not as simple as just relating to his pain.

Let's begin by acknowledging an important starting point: God never wastes a hurt. He's able to take the tangled loose ends of our lives and weave them into something beautiful that brings out the best in us and makes us useful in the lives of other people. But helping has to include more than simply connecting at the point of our pain. When two people who've experienced similar hurts get together, they can certainly understand one another. This creates an instant rapport. They understand deeply what the other person is going through. The challenge is not to equate rapport and understanding with helping.

In 2 Corinthians 1, Paul opens his letter with a statement that can help us understand how to respond appropriately to our pain as we reach out to hurting kids. In verses 3 and 4 he says, "Praise be to the God and Father of our Lord Jesus Christ, the Father of compassion and the God of all comfort, who comforts us in all our troubles, so that we can comfort those in any trouble with the comfort we ourselves have received from God." Paul's point is that it's out of the comfort we've received that we are able to offer comfort to others. Notice it's not merely out of the pain we've suffered. So two people with similar stories of pain can commiserate, but no real healing will occur unless one of the individuals has experienced God's comfort and is able to point the other person to that same hope and healing.

As you think about your past and the pain associated with it, think also about the comfort and compassion you've experienced. Your ministry to hurting kids will come from that comfort. Don't wait for your healing journey to be complete—that won't happen until heaven. Just share what you know is true from your own experience of God's goodness. That will give your words incredible power.

section three

THE NUTS AND BOLTS OF HELPING HURTING KIDS

"THIS IS WHAT THE SOVEREIGN LORD SAYS: WOE TO THE SHEPHERDS OF ISRAEL WHO ONLY TAKE CARE OF THEMSELVES! SHOULD NOT SHEPHERDS TAKE CARE OF THE FLOCK?...YOU HAVE NOT STRENGTHENED THE WEAK OR HEALED THE SICK OR BOUND UP THE INJURED. YOU HAVE NOT BROUGHT BACK THE STRAYS OR SEARCHED FOR THE LOST...THEY WERE SCATTERED BECAUSE THERE WAS NO SHEPHERD.'" —EZEKIEL 34: 2, 4-5

chapter seven

IT'S ALL ABOUT L.O.V.E.

Most hurting kids have nowhere to turn with their pain. The structures that are meant to provide safety and nurture—including the community, the family, the educational system, and even the church—have often failed to provide kids with the support they need to navigate their adolescence successfully. Most of them are left with no choice but to care for themselves and each other. The happy exceptions are students in relationships with trustworthy, nonparental adults who are willing to share their journeys with them—you can be one of these people. And if you choose to take on a hurting adolescent's story, you'll play a vitally important role.

Helping hurting kids is as much about who you are as it is about what you do. The most powerful instrument of ministry you have to offer a student is your own life, lived transparently and honestly so they can see the difference the gospel makes for you. It's all about relationships. Kids' trust in you opens the door to helping them. That's why we need to strive to become the kind of people who are able to offer kids relationships that are beneficial, safe, and life-giving.

It's fine to discuss our own trustworthiness, authenticity, integrity, and availability. But here's where it gets tough: What should you do when a hurting kid unloads a story of pain and brokenness unlike anything you've ever heard before? Or what if he asks for your help with a behavior, emotion, or relationship he can't handle on his own? You can easily feel overwhelmed as the details are shared, and you aren't sure what to do next.

So to get practical, let's talk about the skills a youth worker needs to help hurting kids effectively. Just remember that without a relationship of mutual trust and respect, these skills will be of no value. Our approach must be based on the love we have for the kids we work with.

When a hurting adolescent decides you are trustworthy, she will look for an appropriate time to share her story with you. In most cases disclosures will come informally, spontaneously, and somewhat cautiously, often emerging as a series of installments—each one revealing a bit more of the twisted plot until the whole story can be told. How you respond when a student begins to open up is usually critical to the healing process. Often she begins with a watered-down version of the details—just to see how you'll handle it. If she senses you have the time, the desire, and the patience to hear her out, she'll give you the whole picture.

L.O.V.E.

To make the process a bit easier to remember, let's use the letters in the word love as a framework for thinking through the skills needed to help those kids who invite us into their lives. The methods associated with each letter provide a skill set we need, rather than just a series of consecutive steps to give complete care to kids in pain.

L

The letter "L" concerns *listening*—perhaps the most fundamental skill needed by anyone working with wounded kids. Many teenagers are convinced that no one is listening to them. Everyone is either too busy, preoccupied, stressed, or selfish to give kids the undivided attention they need. We must learn to listen beneath the words—at the level of emotions, nonverbal cues, and even silence. Listening must be active—responsive to what's being said and left unsaid. And of course it must be nonjudgmental. Nothing will shut down a kid's story more quickly than an adult pointing out where he's wrong.

O

"O" refers to what we *offer* students who choose to risk sharing their hearts with us. They've come to us because they believe we have something they need. It's important for us to offer hope in what they often consider to be hopeless circumstances. Offers of encouragement, support, wisdom, and sometimes advice can all express this hope. Maybe the most important thing we can offer kids is the willingness to go deeper with them. Most adults in their lives want to keep things safe and shallow.

V

"V" calls us to *validate* what's happening in the lives of hurting teenagers. Many kids in pain have been told that their perspectives are inaccurate, their emotions are illegitimate, and they need to "get over it." Our relational commitment validates them as people of worth. Our supportive words validate the courage it takes to face their own pain and share their stories. And our patience and gentleness validate the emotions they feel about the circumstances they share with us. The fear, confusion, shame, hurt, isolation, anger, and loss must be processed, not simply stuffed.

E

"E" calls us to quick action, a new perspective, and a deep trust in God. Begin by taking steps to e*liminate immediate dangers*. Many hurting kids are involved in behaviors and relationships that require early intervention. Furthermore, we need to empower adolescents as people with the power to choose. As long as they feel like helpless victims, they won't move forward. But most importantly, we must *expect God* to do his part to accomplish what only he can do in the lives of kids—providing his presence, his comfort, and his healing.

Let's look at each of these L.O.V.E. pieces more closely.

chapter eight

"L" IS FOR LISTEN

Nothing more clearly communicates care for a hurting teenager than thoughtful, active, nonjudgmental listening. Unfortunately, many of us don't do it well. By definition, listening is other-centered, which means it doesn't come naturally. Most of us need to focus on being good listeners if we want the kids we work with to know they matter to us. It's a learned skill that practice sharpens. Listening involves setting aside our own agenda and focusing on the thoughts, emotions, and experiences of another person.

Most people think they're much better listeners than they really are. Don't assume that just because you've heard their words, you've truly listened to a person. And don't forget that unspoken words can be just as important as those spoken. Nonverbal messages communicated through tone of voice, posture, facial expression, and gesture often speak louder than the words themselves. Here are some ways to become more intentional about your listening.

LISTEN BENEATH THE WORDS

As a careful listener, you need to tune in to more than a person's words. By paying attention you can pick up both the content of the spoken message and the deeper nonverbal meaning. As you listen to a student sharing his story, you'll quickly notice that the message comes through on a number of levels. Spoken words are sometimes carefully chosen, and sometimes they become a torrent of thoughts and feelings. These words have significant meaning, especially when they are vented without careful censoring. Particularly listen to the words that describe relationships, emotions, and self-image. A simple sentence such as, "How could I have been that stupid?!" communicates a world of messages about how the teenager sees himself, who he thinks is at fault, how he'll handle similar situations in the future, and how he hopes you'll see him now that you know the truth. When he combines these words with a despairing tone of voice, slumped-forward posture, and his head buried in his hands, the deeper meaning of the message becomes clear. Listening on these deeper levels gives us insights we couldn't possibly gain if we only paid attention to the spoken content of the conversation.

Listening beneath the words involves tuning in to a number of separate messages. If we want students to know they've been fully heard, then being sensitive to all the signals is critical. This can be challenging. At times you'll find that the spoken words say one thing and the nonverbal cues say something completely different. You might hear the words, "It was really no big deal—it didn't bother me at all," but when you observe the body language, pick up the wistful tone of voice, see the eyes cast downward, and hear the carefully measured silence following the statement, you know that what's being said beneath the words is more important than the words themselves.

You should practice tuning in to a few specific things as students share their stories with you. Many of these concern body language.

- Posture is very important to observe. Is it open or closed? Is the student leaning in or pulling away? Is she relaxed or uptight? Is her head held high, or is she looking downward in a posture of shame and brokenness?

- Facial expression is also critical. It takes practice to read another person's face accurately, but what can be learned—especially from the eyes—is critical to understanding the deeper message. A furrowed brow, a hint of a smile, an unblinking eye, pursed lips, breathing pattern—all communicate something at a deeper level and are important to note.

- Tone of voice is another important factor. Interpreting the intonations of voice takes practice, and each kid will have his own unique nuances that you must learn to understand.

I submit to you that the important components of deeper listening concern what is not said.

- The first of these is silence. One of the mistakes many people make is filling the silence instead of letting it speak. In most cases, when a student stops talking, he has a reason. Perhaps he's finding it too painful to go on (a deep breath with a slow exhale and a downward look). Maybe he's practicing what he's about to say by rehearsing it in his mind (blank stare, slight nodding of the head, silently mouthing words, catching himself before he says anything). He could be having an insight that he hasn't had before (faraway look, head moving side to side, even breathing, eyes lighting up in discovery, a little smirk). Don't hesitate to ask a student to interpret the silence for you: "I sense you just had a new thought about this. What was it?"; "It feels like you just hit a wall there—what's keeping you from going on with your story?"; or "I can see you're doing some really good thinking right now. Take your time." Silence can speak volumes. Don't be afraid of it.

- It's important to tune in to another form of unspoken messages—the words a person *doesn't* choose. This often happens when a storyteller is carefully measuring her words. Kids will often use weak words instead of saying what they're really feeling—"frustrated" instead of "angry," "okay, I guess" instead of "awful," "sort of" instead of "exactly." Safe words are usually used to protect the speaker, the listener, or the person being discussed. Whatever the case, take note when a student uses an unexpected word to describe a situation. It may be something you store in the back of your mind for future discussion, or you might want to address it immediately.

LISTEN NONJUDGMENTALLY

Too many adults cast themselves as judge and jury in the lives of teenagers. It's no wonder kids often feel that people only see the bad and never notice the good. If you habitually assume the worst about kids, you will filter their stories through that presupposition and miss much of what they are trying to say. Chances are you're not that kind of person if you're reading this book. Your work with students has allowed you to see the good. You've seen the energy and optimism, the potential, and the dreams. You enjoy kids, and they trust you because you're one of the few adults who don't jump to conclusions.

But listening with acceptance is tough, even for people who enjoy teenagers. Because we have life experience on our side, we can often see where a story is going or what the outcome of certain choices will be. We're tempted to jump in quickly, pass judgment, give our advice, and move on. This approach robs the young person of the opportunity to learn by carefully processing her story. It eliminates the power of self-discovery and the lessons she can learn by slowly and thoughtfully working through the problem-solving sequence. Teenagers are a lot smarter than we acknowledge them to be. The nonjudgmental adult allows kids to exercise wisdom as they learn from their own experiences.

An accepting listener waits for the speaker to tell the whole story. Most of the stories you hear from students will have more than one side. Students typically tell their stories in pieces, unwrapping one layer at a time. We can easily jump to conclusions without hearing the whole thing and diminish the learning potential in the process. Assume there's more to the story. Patiently wait for the details to emerge. Look for opportunities to hear another angle from someone else. Don't assume that your student's version is the only one you need to hear.

When we listen without judgment, we consciously give kids the benefit of the doubt. Instead of hearing the story in the worst possible light, we assume the best. The world is a hostile place for a lot of kids. Many of the cultural constructs in their lives exist to control and manage them. Instead of protecting kids from their communities, our system protects communities from kids (though there are good reasons why this has become necessary). When we choose to give kids the benefit of the doubt, we become rare exceptions in a world that typically assumes the worst.

Nonjudgmental listening doesn't give quick advice. Kids often interpret steps and formulas as adult arrogance. You might see a quick solution to a kid's problem. Or the next steps might be obvious to your adult mind. But responding in a "top-down" way—sharing those next steps—often communicates that we weren't really listening to the heart. When kids share their stories, they're looking for more than solutions—they want comfort and care, they need empathy and compassion. Advice bypasses those more costly gifts and provides the quick response instead.

LISTEN ACTIVELY

Listening is conversational. Lack of attention or eye contact, bored looks, abruptly changing the subject, needing a question repeated—all those behaviors show someone you're not really listening. A teenager who may already struggle with feelings of insignificance, shame, and guilt will interpret this as personal rejection. Active listening takes time, energy, and practice.

At some point in our lives, most adults have experienced

the comfort of being really listened to. We fondly recall those conversations because we felt so deeply cared for by the person who hung on our every word; kept eye contact; asked to have more information; turned the conversation back to us with thoughtful questions; and let us know that they heard not only our words, but also the feelings beneath them. But most kids rarely experience what it feels like to be deeply heard.

To listen actively you must consciously take the attention off yourself and focus on the other person. The responses you offer to the kid while he's sharing his story will either make your listening active or passive. Begin by thinking about your posture. Position yourself so you're facing the person, make eye contact, lean forward to communicate attention, put down what you're doing, smile. Of course this all sounds cheesy when you read it in a book, but an attentive listener behaves this way. Nod your head and allow your face to communicate appropriate emotion. Verbal responses such as, "Really?" "Tell me more," "What happened then?" and "How were you feeling?" can really let a kid know you're tracking with him.

Active listening involves reflecting back to the storyteller what you're hearing—both verbally and emotionally. Let the person know what you're hearing him say and check for accuracy. Active listeners ask questions that invite further disclosure and let the other person know he's acceptable and his story matters.

Obviously, active listening is tough work. It takes a lot more time than quick responses of advice giving or clichéd answers. It requires conscious engagement with someone else's words and emotions—something that doesn't come easily to most people. And it takes practice. The best way to show most hurting kids that you love them is to take the time to listen.

Ralph Nichols said it well in *Are You Listening?*: "The most basic of all human needs is the need to understand and be understood. The best way to understand people is to listen to them."

ACTIVE LISTENING SKILLS

Practice these skills to become a better listener. They'll pay off not only in your work with hurting kids but also in all your other important relationships.

1. **Attending, acknowledging**—providing verbal or nonverbal connection with the other (in other words, eye contact, open posture, nodding, uh-huhs).

2. **Restating, paraphrasing**—responding to a person's basic verbal message by saying it in your own words.

3. **Reflecting**—bouncing back feelings, experiences, or content that has been heard or perceived through verbal and nonverbal cues.

4. **Interpreting**—offering a tentative explanation about the other's feelings, desires, or meanings.

5. **Summarizing, synthesizing**—bringing together feelings and experiences in some way, and providing a big-picture perspective.

6. **Probing**—questioning in a supportive way that requests more information or attempts to clear up confusions.

7. **Giving feedback**—sharing perceptions of the other's ideas or feelings; or if appropriate, disclosing relevant personal information.

8. **Supporting**—showing warmth and caring.

9. **Checking perceptions**—finding out with good questions if your interpretations and perceptions are valid and accurate.

10. **Being quiet**—giving the other time to think, as well as talk.

Adapted from Marisue Pickering, "Communication," EXPLORATIONS, A Journal of Research of the University of Maine 3, no. 1 (Fall 1986): 16-19.

chapter nine

"O" IS FOR OFFER

Love is more than listening. Love takes the initiative; it makes the first move; and it offers hope, encouragement, and support. Love chooses risks that seem unreasonable to the casual observer. If we want to communicate real love in our relationships with hurting kids, we'll find ways to *offer ourselves* to them—sometimes even before they ask. A freely given gift means so much more than something demanded or requested—it powerfully communicates, not only about the giver, but also about the receiver.

As youth workers we have chosen to offer ourselves to students. We give them our time and energy. We share experiences and create memories together. Our lives are openly lived so kids can learn from our stories. When kids are hurting, their needs increase and our involvement in their lives becomes even more strategic. You have some specific gifts you can offer hurting kids who choose to share their pain with you.

OFFER HOPE

You can usually count on the fact that when a hurting student comes for help, she's probably exhausted most of her options. Adolescents work hard to establish independence, so they'll frequently try to solve things on their own or with their friends before they'll open up to an adult. When this happens, chances are good that they've lost hope. The problems of adolescence are complex—sometimes too complex for adults to figure out. It's no wonder kids lose perspective.

What does hope look like for a kid who has lost it? Hope

provides a new perspective—it offers a look forward. Hope repaints a picture of the future. Many adolescents who find themselves in painful circumstances have slipped into survival mode. That means they live only for the moment, simply trying to make it through the day. It's hard for them to think about the future when the present is unbearable. This is when the new point of view that you have to offer a student can help.

As an objective optimistic friend, you can see the bigger picture. You've seen other kids struggling with similar issues and finding their way to health. You've seen what God has done in your own life. Your perspective comes from further down the road, and you can offer hope to the student who can't see it from where he is. The challenge: Make sure you don't promise false hope. It's too easy to say things like, "Don't worry; everything will turn out just fine"; "If you change the way you relate to your dad, he'll change the way he talks to you"; or "You'll make new friends, and they'll be a lot better than those losers you've been hanging around with."

Moving forward is often a struggle, and it's important not to pretend otherwise. Base the hope you offer on God's goodness and the safety he offers with his presence. If the circumstances causing the young person's pain involve the choices of others (parents, siblings, coaches, teachers, friends), you can't guarantee that the others will change. But if you have known God to be good, you can help the hurting kid cling to that truth. I've often said to hurting teenagers, "You can be a healthy person even though you're surrounded by people who aren't." The challenge, of course, is accomplishing that goal without having any healthy people to lean on—which brings up the next gift we can offer hurting kids.

OFFER SUPPORT AND ENCOURAGEMENT

Hurting kids have a tough time trying to change their lives all by themselves. Ecclesiastes 4:10 says, "If one falls down, his friend can help him up. But pity the man who falls and has no one to help him up!" We need each other. When kids ask us to help them work through situations, they're asking for more than our words of advice. They need a companion. Kids realize that without someone to accompany them on their journeys, the chances of long-term success dramatically reduce. Most of the credible self-help programs with good track records of success—Alcoholics Anonymous and Weight Watchers, for example—are based on the fundamental concept of the shared journey. After acknowledging that change is necessary, the first step toward recovery is admitting that it can't be done alone. To a teenager in pain, we can offer our presence on the journey.

We begin by offering kids our time. If you work with students as a coach, teacher, small group leader, or mentor, proactively communicate your availability. Kids are reluctant to intrude into the lives of adults. They often have the impression that we don't have time for them, so they're cautious about asking for time unless we've found ways to let them know we're available. I've done this by creating a small card that says, THIS COUPON IS GOOD FOR A SODA AND AN HOUR OF MY UNDIVIDED ATTENTION—CALL ME WHEN YOU NEED ME. My name and phone number are on the card, and I make sure the kids in my group each have one. That way they don't feel as if they're infringing on my life when they ask for some time. Most often they just say, "Hey, I'd like to cash in my soda coupon sometime this week." It's a great way to open the door.

As kids share their stories and we help them find paths toward wholeness, they'll need more than just our time. They may be frightened to face secrets that have been buried for years. But trying to break habitual patterns is hard work. This is when you offer encouragement. You become a cheerleader on the sideline, urging them on and letting them know you believe in them. You can't do it for them, but you can support them as they go. Encouragement can be communicated in so many practical ways. A quick phone call to remind a hurting kid that you're praying for her (especially on a particularly tough day) will mean the world to her. Sometimes you may find it fun (and timesaving) to call when you know she's not home and leave a message on her voice mail. You can also send a quick text message to her cell phone, an e-mail, or even an old-fashioned, handwritten card to let a kid know she's not in this alone. And when you're actually with her in person, a few well-chosen words of encouragement always go a long way.

The word *encourage* means to fill someone up with courage. Facing one's pain and taking responsibility for unhealthy responses to it require an immense amount of courage. Healing runs on the fuel of encouragement. Keep kids' tanks full by intentionally encouraging them any way you can.

Time and encouragement are great, but you have more to offer a student who's on the road to health and wholeness—accountability. Without it, the journey could be much tougher. As kids face their pain, they learn to respond differently than they have in the past. They'll take relational risks, break old habits, and replace destructive patterns with healthy ones. The accountability you offer kids as they take these courageous steps often serves to keep them on track. Provide accountability by simply holding kids responsible for the commitments they make. You won't play an umpire role—calling kids out when they fail—but a coaching role, gently correcting missteps so they can eventually develop a consistent life. I've held kids accountable for doing their homework, their Internet use, avoiding substance abuse, keeping moral purity in dating relationships, personal quiet times, limiting self-injury, and even committing not to take their own lives. It means checking up regularly—not like a cop—but like a genuine friend who wants the very best for them.

You can offer kids who are struggling one more gift of support and encouragement. They desperately need this on their journey toward healing, and most of the teenagers you work with rarely experience it—the gift of grace, forgiveness, and second chances. Kids will mess up in spite of their best intentions. This is when your support is more important than ever. For most teenagers, failure means rejection. The most loving thing we can do is offer them relationship and support in the face of failure. Remember: Don't make light of the failure or pretend it didn't happen. Rather pick them up, dust them off, and help them find the right direction again. When you offer a struggling teenager a second chance, you model the very nature of God to him. The book of Hosea provides a wonderful picture of God giving his people second (and third and fourth) chances. For kids who are learning to deal with their pain in more constructive ways, our goal is not to help them establish a failure-free path, but to teach them how to start over after they've failed. The most powerful way to tell a kid, "I forgive you," is through our actions, not our words.

Just so you know—this is the hardest part of loving wounded kids. Imagine you've poured your life into a struggling teenager, and now you've finally seen him making some good choices and his future looks bright. Suddenly, you watch him crash and burn before your very eyes. You easily can feel as though *you're* the failure. At this point most adults give up on kids. They want to make an investment where the dividends are more consistent. If you can hang on with a struggling kid, your ministry will be rare and precious. Remember: We often don't see the results of our work for years. Be patient, be forgiving, and be loving—it'll mean the world to the hurting kids you know.

OFFER TO GO DEEPER

Most hurting kids tend to keep their conversations and relationships safe and shallow. To go deeper means to expose secrets, reveal our flaws, and risk rejection. Unfortunately, rearranging things at the surface doesn't bring about lasting change in the life of a hurting kid. Sometimes we realize we have no choice but to go deeper. Most kids' problems are emotional ("I'm—sad, depressed, lonely, afraid, angry"); behavioral ("I'm—addicted to drugs, cutting myself, puking after every meal, having sex with my girlfriend"); or relational ("I—don't get along with my parents, just broke up with my boyfriend, am not sure if God could love me").

Because these issues are quite visible, we're tempted to simply do a quick, surface fix. We write prescriptions (by the millions) to change kids' emotions, or we tell them to snap out of it. We condemn inappropriate behaviors and exhort kids to change. (To the anorexic: "Just start eating, for crying out loud!" To the pornography addict: "Just stop watching, for crying out loud!") And we belittle the relational pain kids feel. ("Get over it; life's tough." Or "There are lots more guys where he came from.") Or, worst of all, we spiritualize the whole thing. ("All things work together for good," or " Jesus knew what it felt like to be rejected.")

Most of the kids you work with have enough insight to know that clichés and behavioral rearrangements are not enough to bring lasting change—and that "snapping out of it" doesn't work for deep, painful emotions. I've learned that teenagers are often more willing to face the deeper issues in their lives than adults are. The honesty of a kid who is willing to look deep is refreshing and should be affirmed.

WHY YOUR INVOLVEMENT IS SO CRITICAL

First, going deeper is unfamiliar. Kids live in the moment. They experience life as a series of consecutive, isolated events. With their new, emerging ability to think in an abstract and integrated way, they can now weave the experiences of their lives into coherent personal histories. Because this is a new capacity, adolescents need guides to take them on the inward journeys. Left on their own, they'll come up with some distorted interpretations of what they find. An objective, loving companion who can help a kid sort through the mess of his memories will keep him from coming to inappropriate assumptions about what his past says about him.

Second, going deeper is scary. Kids know something intense and probably painful underlies their issues, and they're afraid they might find more than they can bear on their own. "What if I find something I can't handle?" kids typically ask when you encourage them to look beneath the surface.

Kids know that in order to find real hope for the future, they need to look at what the Bible calls the "inner parts" (Psalm 51:6). Every teenager you know has a deep thirst for unconditional love, a hunger for significance, and a longing to belong. God put these desires at the core of each human being as a way of drawing us to himself. Most kids have experienced disappointment in all three areas because humans naturally try to find fulfillment in ways that don't involve God. "You can do it on your own, and you can have satisfaction right now" is the lie kids live with. Desperate attempts to be lovable or significant, as well as frantic efforts to belong, often cause kids to make destructive choices with disastrous outcomes. If you can gently take an adolescent to the place where she's willing to face those areas of thirst and longing, you can begin to point her in the direction of true satisfaction. Simply rearranging surface issues will rob kids of knowing the deep joy of having God meet their most core needs.

TAKING THE CONVERSATION DEEPER WITH OPEN-ENDED QUESTIONS

Open-ended questions encourage people to talk about what's important to them. They ask for people's opinions and ideas on a topic. Open-ended questions don't have right answers. They help to increase understanding, gather information, and open unexplored territory. Open-ended questions often elicit unexpected responses. Because open-ended questions are not leading, they invite others to tell their stories in their own words. Use open-ended questions frequently, though not exclusively, in conversation. When asking open-ended questions, prepare for anything and be willing to listen to the responses.

Some examples of open-ended questions—

- What does it feel like to live at your house?
- Would you tell me about the first time it happened?
- Why do you think you responded that way?
- How do you think the other people who were there felt?
- How are you different from each of your siblings?
- What's the best thing that happened to you today?
- If you had it to do all over again, would you do anything differently?
- Where have you seen God show up in your story?

chapter ten
"V" IS FOR VALIDATE

Love listens and offers hope, support, and relational depth. And in the process, it validates the one being loved. When we validate someone, we affirm his credibility and authenticate his identity. We tell him he's real and believable. Let's remember that adolescents are focused on answering key questions about identity: *Who am I? Where do I fit? What is my contribution? What are my personal strengths and weaknesses? Do people like me? What do I need to change to be more acceptable?* Kids constantly monitor the people around them to get these questions answered. Relational pain and deep hurt erode a kid's positive self-perception. As he tries to make sense of the things that happen to him, he often answers identity questions in the most negative possible way. "I am a loser. I really don't fit anywhere. I have no contribution to make. There's no reason for people to like me. I've tried a bunch of things to make myself more likable, and most of them have just made things worse."

If you leave these negative assumptions unchallenged, they will soon become the basis for adulthoods of compensating, camouflaging, and controlling—often with relationally disastrous outcomes. When kids take the risk of sharing their pain with us, we have a unique opportunity to affirm the positive things we see. Obviously, in these moments of disclosure, kids are the most vulnerable. They've dropped their guard, shared their weaknesses, and told you they need you. Rejection by a trusted adult at this point will simply reinforce their negative feelings. Loving acceptance challenges everything negative that kids are beginning to believe about themselves. Validating hurting kids is one of the most strategic and significant things we can do for them. Here are some specific ways you can validate hurting teenagers who choose to share their stories with you.

VALIDATE THEIR COURAGE

Opening up to another person can be dangerous and frightening for most teenagers. When that person is an adult, sharing becomes even scarier. Young people make assumptions about the willingness—or, more accurately, unwillingness—of adults to hear their stories. Many kids have experience with adults who belittle, ignore, or reject what's going on in teenagers' lives. That obviously will make them reluctant to let you in.

When a kid shares a struggle with you, you can safely assume that she needed a significant amount of trust and courage to do this. Living courageously is good and should be affirmed. Learn to accept the trust of an adolescent as an honor, and express your gratitude as you would for any costly gift you receive. Let her know you understand that what she's doing isn't easy and that you're thankful she trusts you with this situation.

It's important to validate the courage of kids not only as they begin to open up but also throughout the process as they continue to take greater and greater risks. It takes courage to acknowledge disappointment. When you see a young person honestly facing a hard-to-control emotion such as fear or sadness, you need to encourage him along the way. Say things like, "I can only imagine how hard it is for you to talk about the sadness you feel over what's going on between your mom and dad right now—I really respect your willingness to face it as honestly as you are. You're doing a really gutsy thing, and I feel honored to have you share it with me."

Validating the courage of a kid who has chosen to take a risk can strengthen him for other risks that will undoubtedly be part of his journey toward healing. You want to affirm character qualities that will lead to a healthy, confident adulthood, and choosing courage is one of the most important. Often courage has a lot to do with the way kids handle their emotions.

VALIDATE THEIR EMOTIONS

Most kids have a pretty good idea of which emotions are acceptable and which aren't. In many cases kids have been told how they ought to feel in certain circumstances. So when they experience any emotions that don't fit neatly into that range of acceptability, they often hesitate to allow themselves to feel those emotions. "There must be something wrong with me," they assume.

Furthermore, they may not know what to do with negative or painful emotions simply because no one has ever taught them how to process those feelings appropriately. All of this happens at a time in their developmental journeys when emotional awareness is sharply increasing. Imagine the dilemma this creates for kids. Inside they have bubbling cauldrons of intense and very real emotions, yet kids constantly evaluate these feelings to determine whether or not they're acceptable and what to do with them.

You can do something to diffuse much of the tension surrounding the issue of emotions for kids in pain. Simply give them permission to feel what they're feeling. If they know they can relax and allow themselves to experience whatever emotions they're having, they'll feel free to process these emotions honestly. Let them know you're okay with anger, tears, and confusion, or with excitement, joy, and elation. When we can release kids from the responsibility of censoring their emotions, they can begin to be honest about what's really going on inside.

Let kids know that how they feel about situations is appropriate and acceptable. It's proper to feel hurt when their friends gossip about them. It's okay to be afraid to go home when their dads abuse them. It's understandable that they'd feel angry with a teacher who humiliates them in front of the class. When a person allows an emotion to come to the surface, she can feel, understand, and express it in an appropriate way.

When kids don't know how to handle their emotions in healthy ways, they may respond with coping strategies that usually create more problems. These responses tend to fall into one of three categories:

1. Stuff it—emotional energy is real and can't be ignored. When hurting kids believe that feeling a particular emotion is taboo, they still have to do something with it. Many of them develop the habit of simply burying their emotions. They would say they ignore their emotions, but the only way to do this is to shove the feelings into a secluded corner of their hearts. Ignoring a feeling doesn't defuse it. In fact, stuffed emotions often flare up and are wildly out of proportion to the event that sparked them—like a bursting balloon, they can explode into reality at the slightest provocation. But most of the time, stuffed emotions just fester in the soul, gradually eroding a kid from the inside out and forcing him into a hollow, contrived existence where nothing is real. Obviously, burying emotions isn't a great way to manage them.

2. Cover it up—sometimes emotions just can't be buried. They are too intense, too painful, and too consuming to be ignored. When this happens, many kids learn the fine art of camouflage. This relatively simple strategy involves creating another, more intense emotion than the one they really feel and focusing on that one instead. Anger camouflages sadness, the thrill of an adrenaline rush masks fear, and a moment of sexual euphoria covers up a lifetime of loneliness. The contrived emotion can be controlled and managed, unlike the deeper emotion that leaves the kid feeling helpless.

3. Indiscriminately act it out—this is basically venting, and it's often the most destructive response. A person who is acting out will intensely express the emotion with no regard for how it may impact anyone. You've probably seen kids do this, alienating their friends and anyone else who gets in their way. Venting becomes a vicious, self-destructive cycle: The more a person vents, the more other people pull away; the angrier a person becomes, the more she frantically vents, and so on. Kids in this mode not only need others to validate their emotions but also to learn to think through how their expressions of emotion will affect others.

HOW TO ACCEPT AND REJECT EMOTIONS

Ways to Reject Emotions

These responses say, "How you feel really doesn't matter."

- Advise/solve: "What I think you ought to do is…" or "It seems to me that all you need to do is…"

- Disdain/belittle: "I can't see any reason why you'd feel…" or "There really is no reason to feel…"

- Correct/teach: "What I think you're actually feeling is…" or "I don't think you're feeling…"

Ways to Validate Emotions

These responses say, "Tell me more about how you feel."

- Reflect: "It sounds like what you're feeling is…" or "What I'm hearing you say is…"

- Clarify: "Are you saying that you felt…" or "I'm wondering if you are feeling any…"

- Extend: "Did you also feel any…" or "If I were in your shoes, I'd probably feel _____."

VALIDATE THEIR WORTH

When painful things happen in the lives of adolescents, they will often assume it's somehow their fault. Children of divorce, rape victims, survivors of sexual abuse, and children of alcoholics all seem to share this trait, believing that somehow they are responsible for the awful things that happen to them. In some cases the people who caused their pain actually told them it's their fault. Sadly, this is very common in cases of abuse, alcoholism, and family breakdown. When a kid has been told he caused his mom to drink, a divorce to happen, or a sexual assault, persuading him otherwise can be very difficult. Heaping blame on top of the pain these kids already feel is a particularly cruel form of abuse. When this happens, kids end up feeling defective and worthless. They desperately need relational validation from a loving adult who wants to release them from lives of self-loathing and brokenness.

It's relatively easy to understand that kids who've been told they're bad will struggle with self-esteem. But, surprisingly, kids will also assume responsibility for their pain without someone else placing the blame on them. They decide to blame themselves. This distorted assumption has a reason, and if you understand it, you can help kids through their pain in ways that few others will be able to.

All humans are naturally predisposed to keep their lives as pain-free as possible. Most teenagers make this a high priority. As they work through the painful realities in their lives, they believe that if they can just figure out what happened to cause all this grief, perhaps they could learn to avoid it in the future. Assuming personal responsibility for our hurt is a subtle but powerful way of creating a sense of control in pain management. Oftentimes, this way of thinking leads to lifestyles of frantic perfectionism, paranoia, compulsive compliance, and other forms of drivenness that can become all consuming. When we reassure kids that what happened wasn't their fault, we free them to face their pain courageously and find appropriate ways to embrace healing.

Dealing with a teenager who feels unlovable, defective, and relationally unworthy requires more than words to move her forward. You validate the worth of broken kids by the way you relate to them. When you offer them time, support, encouragement, respect, and trust, you force kids to look at themselves in brand-new ways. Kids usually don't know how to respond to your love. They will push you away, even though you know they desperately long for what you're offering. Your love challenges their sense of personal defectiveness, and they're just not sure what to do with that. Be patient. Understand that for a wounded teenager to accept your love also means that she has to accept the idea that she's lovable. That means giving up control and becoming vulnerable in ways that have usually led to pain in the past.

Ask God to give you eyes to see the beauty and potential of each young person you work with. There is great dignity in being image bearers of the Creator. Validate the worth of a teenager by helping him see his potential, by affirming the positive character traits you see in him, by celebrating his successes, by forgiving his failures, and by offering him unconditional friendship.

chapter eleven

"E" IS FOR ELIMINATE, EMPOWER, AND EXPECT

We've talked about expressing our love through active listening, offering ourselves to kids in a variety of practical ways, and validating kids by relating to them as people of dignity and worth. A few final factors will round out our work with hurting kids. Fortunately for this acrostic, they all start with "E." Each is an important component of the help we offer kids and must be intentionally woven into the healing journey.

ELIMINATE IMMEDIATE DANGERS

Wounded kids often find dangerous and destructive ways to handle their hurt. Substance abuse, eating disorders, promiscuous sexual behavior, self-mutilation, gang membership, violence, criminal activity, running away from home, addictions, and a variety of other inappropriate choices may begin to emerge as kids try to cope with increasing pain. Because they feel immortal ("It can't possibly happen to me"), they often engage in blatantly high-risk behaviors without recognizing the potential harm they might bring on themselves. In many cases parents—even good ones—are oblivious to what their kids are involved in and may not be in good positions to find out the truth. Very few adults are welcome in the secret world of teenagers.

As kids develop a growing trust in you, they'll gradually let you share some of their secrets—some that even their closest friends may not know. This gives you a unique and important responsibility. In the simplest terms, you could have the opportunity to save kids from themselves. As an objective adult you're able to see the immediate dangers to which kids expose themselves. And as someone they trust, you may be able to protect them from further harm by challenging them to take intentional steps toward safety as soon as possible. Some of the kids you'll work with have felt so ignored and alone, they now believe they must resort to extreme behaviors to get attention. Don't ignore attention-seeking behavior. You need to answer this cry for help.

In some cases this will require radical and even unwelcome intervention. When kids are on dangerous or self-destructive paths, they may be unwilling or unable to provide for their own safety. This means you might have to do it for them. Kids may need to be removed from dangerous situations. Report these cases to the appropriate authorities (starting with your supervisor) and provide whatever support is needed. Some teenagers may need hospitalization before they self-destruct. Involve a doctor in the process and ensure kids' safety even though they may resist. If a kid is suicidal, intensify your care for her and do everything in your power to remove the means of suicide she has chosen—have her give you the pills or the gun. If she's unwilling to cooperate, use whatever means are necessary to care for her.

Some situations aren't as intense as those described above, but they will require swift intervention as well. For example, kids who are caught up in drug or alcohol abuse, involved in illegal activities, or participating in dangerous sexual behaviors are all vulnerable to consequences they may not even be aware of. Of course, you know these problems are deeper than their surface symptoms and that it will take some time to get to the bottom of their stories. Addressing the immediate dangers doesn't downplay the importance of going deep with kids, but it simply recognizes that some issues need to be taken care of first to ensure that no further damage occurs. Make it your first priority to identify and eliminate these factors. Kids won't always cooperate. But if they're asking for your help, eliminating dangers should be the first order of business.

Recognize that when you ask kids to give up some of these potentially hazardous behaviors and relationships, they'll need your support and encouragement. Some of the things you'll challenge them to walk away from are physiologically or psychologically addictive. Be patient, be firm, and be supportive. As kids consider their decisions to eliminate harmful habits from their lives, you'll need to remind them that they are "choosers"—they are responsible for their own decisions and are able to take responsibility for their actions.

EMPOWER CHOICE

A key component of our humanness is our volitional capacity. Our ability to choose gives us dignity and allows us to participate in meaningful relationships. Sometimes kids with wounded spirits forget that they're choosers. Their experiences have told them that things happen to them. They often report feeling like insignificant corks bobbing helplessly down a river they have no control over. Life just happens, and the best they can hope for is to find ways to survive. This helpless feeling robs them of the joy of being fully alive.

We empower kids as choosers when we hold them responsible for their choices. We're tempted to leave those kids who've been wounded in victim mode and simply protect them from further harm. While it's important to provide comfort and kindness to hurting kids, we do them no favors by allowing them to feel sorry for themselves and to continue to use their circumstances as excuses for living as victims.

Kids must be reminded that in all of life's circumstances, they have options. Some options will lead to healthy outcomes, others will lead to unhealthy ones. The ability to see the connection between choices and outcomes is critical in helping kids move toward true wholeness. When a kid loses the sense of that connection, he can begin to feel he's no longer responsible for what happens. After all, he didn't make a choice—it just happened. This approach simply leads to more feelings of helplessness and an unwillingness to own the capacity to choose.

Sometimes a correct choice may seem more costly in the short-term, but it will lead to a positive outcome down the road. Sometimes it's hard for kids who are holding on by a thread to make those kinds of tough choices without the support and encouragement you can provide. It's especially tough to hold kids responsible for the ways in which they cope with their pain when they've been deeply hurt by the other people in their lives. We find it easy to justify the survival strategies that kids put in place, but we need to help kids resist the temptation to allow those patterns to become habitual.

The bottom line: Unless we're willing to do the difficult work of helping kids come to terms with their capacity as choosers, they're destined to live as helpless victims, disengaged from the realities of life around them and unable to feel that they have a part in writing their own life stories.

EXPECT GOD'S INVOLVEMENT

Here's the good news: As you get involved in the lives of these kids, whom God has entrusted to your care, you will quickly recognize your abject inadequacy for the task before you. It doesn't matter if you're a Ph.D. or a high school grad; before long you'll realize that your human wisdom is not enough to help kids sort through the complexities of their lives. It's best for us to assume the role of apprentices. Isaiah tells us that God's name, among other things, is "Wonderful Counselor" (Isaiah 9:6). He knows the needs of the kids we work with, and he loves them more consistently than we ever will. He knows exactly what they need to get their lives back on track, and he's committed to providing it for them. Amazingly, he often chooses us to be the deliverers of his love and wisdom. We get into trouble when we begin to believe that we're doing it on our own.

Paul says it well in 1 Corinthians 1:26-29: "Think of what you were when you were called. Not many of you were wise by human standards; not many were influential; not many were of noble birth. But God chose the foolish things of the world to shame the wise; God chose the weak things of the world to shame the strong. He chose the lowly things of this world and the despised things—and the things that are not— to nullify the things that are, so that no one may boast before him." You see, God puts us in situations that are over our heads so that when good things happen, we will recognize our dependence on him and live lives of humble service.

When we make ourselves available to hurting kids in God's name, we can expect his involvement on a number of significant levels:

- First, we can count on him to give us what we need to be effective in our roles as his apprentices. Proverbs 3:5 says, "Trust in the Lord with all your heart and lean not on your own understanding." According to James 1:5, God will give us wisdom if we ask him for it. When we find ourselves in situations that need divine wisdom, we can be confident in its availability to us—we simply need to ask. Furthermore, if we operate in dependence on God, the fruits of his Spirit will be evident in our relationships with hurting kids. Love, patience, kindness, gentleness, and even self-control (Galatians 5:22-23)—all communicate God's character through us. Expect God's presence with you as you represent him in the lives of hurting kids. The apostle Paul's secret in Philippians 4:13 is simple: "I can do everything through him who gives me strength."

- Second, expect God's presence with the hurting kids you work with. He can be trusted to be the good God of compassion and comfort to hurting kids. God gives kids the courage to face the tough realities they'd rather ignore. God offers his presence to kids when life is hopelessly lonely. God provides comfort when circumstances make it too painful to go on. This reassures us when we can't physically be there with a kid who is going through a particularly rough time. Philippians 4:19 reminds us that "God will meet all your needs according to his glorious riches in Christ Jesus."

God's involvement powerfully encourages each of us as we help kids on their journey toward wholeness. The prerequisite for calling kids to a deep trust in God is to have known his goodness in our own lives. When we've felt his healing touch, heard his words of encouragement, and rested in his presence, we can passionately call kids to the same. Frankly, I'm glad we don't have to do this on our own.

GOD'S PROMISES TO HURTING KIDS
- PSALM 50:15: "CALL UPON ME IN THE DAY OF TROUBLE; I WILL DELIVER YOU."
- PSALM 68:6: "GOD SETS THE LONELY IN FAMILIES, HE LEADS FORTH THE PRISONERS WITH SINGING."
- ISAIAH 41:10 (NASB): "DO NOT ANXIOUSLY LOOK ABOUT YOU, FOR I AM YOUR GOD. I WILL STRENGTHEN YOU."
- HOSEA 14:4: "I WILL HEAL THEIR WAYWARDNESS AND LOVE THEM FREELY."
- HEBREWS 13:5 (NASB): "I WILL NEVER DESERT YOU, NOR WILL I EVER FORSAKE YOU."
- 1 JOHN 1:9: "IF WE CONFESS OUR SINS, HE IS FAITHFUL AND JUST AND WILL FORGIVE US OUR SINS."

When you find yourself asking what to do with a hurting kid—just remember to "L.O.V.E." him. That means listening with your eyes and heart, as well as your ears. It means offering hope, encouragement, and depth. It means validating kids' worth by acknowledging their courage and affirming what's going on for them emotionally. And of course it means protecting them by eliminating danger from their lives, empowering them as choosers, and expecting God to do his part in bringing about the healing you long to see occurring in kids' lives.

chapter twelve

MISTAKES THAT CAN DESTROY YOUR MINISTRY WITH HURTING KIDS

In my years spent working with kids and youth workers, I've heard too many stories about well-meaning people making ministry blunders—they just weren't thinking. Each of the following points represents a story or two where major damage was done to a youth ministry, a church, a family, or an individual kid because someone blew it. Learn from the mistakes of others and avoid falling into a trap that could disqualify you from the work you love doing with kids and their families.

AVOID BEING ALONE WITH A KID (SUSPICIONS AND MISUNDERSTANDINGS)

Your organization may have policies regarding this important issue. Unfortunately, those policies are based on the fact that a small percentage of people cannot be trusted when they're alone with children or teenagers. It's not about whether you see yourself as a threat to kids–suspicion or a false accusation can sink your ministry with hurting kids almost as quickly as an actual violation. Please be careful! If some sort of accusation were to be brought against you, having a well-established track record of taking extra care in this area will help you. For many of us, these prohibitions make our efforts to legitimately care for kids much more difficult. But at this point in history we simply have no choice.

Some of the practical implications—

- Don't have one-on-one meetings with kids in your home. And when you're dealing with the opposite sex, make it a rule. You should have no reason to make exceptions.

It's great to have students in your home, as long as other people are there to provide accountability and ensure that nothing inappropriate occurs.

- Don't be alone in your car with just one student. If a kid needs a ride home, take a whole group along, if possible, or have another adult ride with you to provide accountability.

- Be careful on retreats and other youth group events. Two-person tents, long walks in the woods, and other private times can be easily misunderstood.

- If you meet in an office, ensure that there's an uncovered window in the door. If not, keep the door ajar. And restrict your meetings to times when other people are around.

You may also want to consider some of the following options when pursuing meaningful conversations with kids.

- Arrange to meet in a restaurant, coffee shop, mall food court, or some other public location.

- Go for a walk together and stick to open, visible places.

- If a student stops by your house when you're alone, talk outside on the porch, on the deck, or in the yard.

Think about ways to build in these precautions as natural parts of your ministry. Don't make a big deal out of them with the kids. And take extra care not to give students the impression that they are untrustworthy or dangerous, causing you to take these steps.

BEING CARELESS WITH PHYSICAL TOUCH

We all know that healthy affection is one of the key missing ingredients in many kids' lives today. With fragile families and busy or absent parents, a lot of kids miss out on this important developmental asset. Some people have speculated that the absence of appropriate physical touch can cause kids to look for it in a variety of unhealthy ways. This can lead to the sexualizing of even the most innocent interactions. In some cases the only types of physical touch these children have known are inappropriate. For them, touch has been abusive, coercive, demanding, manipulative, controlling, or damaging in some other way. The bottom line is that a young person can badly misunderstand touch. What may seem like appropriate physical contact to you—a hand on the knee, a quick hug, holding hands during a prayer, an arm around the shoulder—can confuse a kid who's had distorted experiences with touch in her past.

The fact that we have to talk about this topic is another sad reality of working with kids today. We can't predict how our touch will be interpreted. Typically these kids' wounds, which created this confusion in the first place, are invisible. The student may give no immediate reaction to indicate there is a problem. As a general rule, avoid physical contact of any kind—particularly in the early stages of a relationship with any kid. As the trust in your relationship grows, you may feel comfortable introducing appropriate physical interactions. Obviously, touch should be used to communicate only positive messages—"Good job," "I care about you," "I understand your pain," "Congratulations," "You're awesome," and so on.

Be very sensitive to nonverbal cues that say, "Please don't touch." Ask yourself, *Am I touching this kid for my sake or for his?* And if you decide to use any kind of touch, be very careful to use only blatantly nonsexual contact—a side hug, a pat on the back, a squeeze of the shoulder. One more important thing: You should also realize that student-initiated affection isn't necessarily healthy or right. Don't assume that just because a kid is warm and affectionate with you, she's healthy about touch. As the adult it is your responsibility to ensure a safe and healthy environment for every kid—regardless of her intentions.

Currently, educators and ethicists are hotly debating this "touchy" topic, and there are obviously no easy answers. Just be aware that what seems right in the moment may not be right at all. And remember that when you touch a student, you always take a measure of risk.

BEING CARELESS WITH WORDS

We often underestimate the power of words. Don't assume that what you mean to say is what hurting kids actually hear you say. We may be unaware of the loaded meanings of our words. Beware, for instance, of offering false hope. "Everything will be fine" or "Don't worry; it'll all work out" can mean something very different to a despairing kid or a hopeless parent than it does to you.

Also be sensitive in your use of theological language that kids may not understand—especially if they have no church background. Define unfamiliar words and phrases in terms kids can relate to. Concepts like submission, death to self, forgiveness, unconditional love, and unconditional obedience may create confusion because of issues in their backgrounds. The idea of God as a heavenly father may seem very positive to you, but the concept may create fear rather than hope for a kid whose father is a violent alcoholic or a self-serving pedophile. Describing the church as a family is great for kids who have a positive picture of home, but it may immediately cause others to feel excluded and unwelcome.

Perhaps the most important reminder under the heading of "words" regards teasing, sarcasm, put-downs, insults, jokes, and other forms of potentially abusive language. Hurting kids are often not as resilient when it comes to this sort of stuff. Be careful in both your one-on-one interactions and your public conversations. Don't assume that your humor is understood as a joke or that your sarcastic comment is harmless. Hurting kids hang on every word we say, and in their insecurity they will often assume the worst in what they hear.

Just because they put up with verbal jabs from their friends doesn't mean there's no pain involved. Often a hurting kid just assumes that his role is to be the target. So when he hears negative words from us, he quietly absorbs them as just another round of damage he routinely endures.

NOT KNOWING LEGAL RESPONSIBILITIES

When we work with minors, we must take into account a number of legal obligations. These include things like background checks for volunteers, reporting protocols when abuse is suspected or disclosed, record keeping, insurance, reporting criminal activity, and so on. The rules for reporting abuse (covered later in this book) are not the only issues that must be considered. If you have any questions related to the legal side of working with kids, be sure to ask your supervisor for instruction and advice. Regulations differ from region to region, so it would be inappropriate to include all the details in a book like this. Just be sure that you are legally covered with good training, well-developed policies, and insurance coverage for everyone in the organization who works with kids. Willingly submit to the inconvenience of a background check. This simple procedure has identified many high-risk volunteers and saved vulnerable kids from untold hurt.

FOR THE RECORD
YOU NEVER KNOW WHERE A CONVERSATION MIGHT LEAD. WHAT IF SOMEONE ASKS YOU FOR THE DATE WHEN JENNY FIRST TOLD YOU SHE WAS DATE RAPED? OR THEY NEED MORE DETAILS ABOUT THE CONVERSATION WHEN JOHNNY STARTED HINTING AT SUICIDE? KEEPING A RECORD OF YOUR INTERACTIONS WITH KIDS MAY BE A NEW IDEA TO YOU, AND I'M NOT SUGGESTING AN ELABORATE SYSTEM OF NOTES AND FILES. HOWEVER, IT MIGHT BE WORTHWHILE TO FIND A WAY TO DOCUMENT THE IMPORTANT CONVERSATIONS YOU HAVE WITH HURTING KIDS. IF YOU'RE ALREADY A DIARY KEEPER OR YOU

MAINTAIN A DAILY PRAYER LIST, A SIMPLE DATED ENTRY IN YOUR PERSONAL JOURNAL MIGHT BE ENOUGH. IF YOU DON'T REGULARLY WRITE ABOUT YOUR LIFE, IT MIGHT BE WISE TO KEEP A FILE WHERE SIMPLE REMINDER NOTES CAN BE PLACED ON THE LONG SHOT THEY MIGHT BE NEEDED SOMEDAY. IF YOU DO KEEP NOTES, THE CRITICAL ISSUE IS TO ENSURE THAT CONFIDENTIALITY IS GUARANTEED. THAT MEANS CAREFULLY LOCKING UP YOUR FILES AND USING AN INITIAL OR IDENTIFYING NUMBER RATHER THAN EASILY RECOGNIZABLE NAMES IN THE RECORDS.

IGNORING PRIMARY RELATIONSHIPS (MARRIAGE, FAMILY, ADULT FRIENDS)

The best youth workers are those who are not only comfortable in the adult world but also willing to enter the world of teenagers to offer them friendship and ministry. Being comfortable as an adult means treating your marriage, your own children and extended family, and your adult friendships as primary and your relationships with hurting teenagers as secondary. When teenagers (especially hurting kids who feed your need to be needed) begin to displace your spouse, your own kids, or your peers, you quickly lose your platform for ministry.

I cannot stress strongly enough the importance of keeping your marriage and family strong, if you hope to have a significant ministry to hurting kids. I'm not simply talking about guarding your family against intrusion—I'm talking about making an intentional investment. I look with fear and sadness at the story of Eli the high priest who was young Samuel's mentor, but lost his own sons in the process (1 Samuel 1 and 2). He was successful with someone else's son but failed with his own.

We must invest in healthy adult friendships as well. To have an effective ministry with hurting kids, we must ensure that we aren't operating from relational emptiness and hoping these needy students will fill the gaps. Instead we must approach our student relationships with a fullness that comes from healthy friendships and satisfying family relationships.

IGNORING WEAKNESSES AND VULNERABILITIES

If you know (or feel) that you might enter into inappropriate relationships with kids—PLEASE VOLUNTARILY STEP ASIDE FROM WORKING WITH TEENAGERS. This is a sensitive issue and may represent the ultimate example of "preaching to the choir," but my conscience demands that I say it. I've been involved in unraveling too many stories where the damage done in the lives of kids could easily have been avoided had the individual simply possessed the courage to disqualify himself from a potentially dangerous situation.

Each of us knows our own level of weakness (or at least we should, if we hope to be effective with kids). If we truly care about kids, then we'll act in accordance with that knowledge. An alcoholic would be unwise to take a job as a bartender, and a kleptomaniac probably shouldn't work in retail. In the same way, people who find children and teenagers emotionally or sexually arousing should quietly step away from working with them and find a different area in which to expend their ministry energies.

Before you panic, allow me to clarify. Each of us is vulnerable at some level. Our humanness expresses itself in some surprisingly negative ways at times. I'm not talking about the generic predisposition to sin that all of us possess. I'm talking about those of us with a known history of inappropriate interactions with children or youth, with a weakness for pornography, with unresolved gender identity issues, or those who find themselves having sexual thoughts about the children or teenagers they spend time with. Hopefully, a word to the wise is sufficient. There is help for people who are willing to acknowledge a need in these areas. If you find yourself described in these paragraphs, please take the appropriate steps—not only for the sake of kids who will be protected by your courage, but also for the sake of your own growth and health.

section four

WHEN YOU'RE OUT OF YOUR DEPTH: RULES FOR REFERRAL

Sometimes we realize that we just can't deal with a kid's story on our own. This is no cause for shame. Even the most seasoned people-helpers feel unqualified at times. So much of what we encounter when we work with teenagers can't be fixed with a quick formula or a series of simple steps. In many cases there are no easy answers. At times a student simply must be referred.

When I talk about referring a student, I mean you recognize your need for help with a particular situation and invite someone more qualified to share in the responsibility for the teenager or her circumstances. Bottom line—it just means you ask for help when you know you need it.

Many organizations, such as schools, camps, youth clubs, and churches, have very specific rules about when and to whom their employees or volunteers must report certain situations or refer students. **It's important for you to know what these policies are and adhere to them without exception.** If there are no policies or if you're not sure what they are, you'll need to use your best judgment on how to handle tough situations. As a general principle, when you're part of a team that works with kids and you need to ask for help, your first step is to communicate your questions or concerns to the person in the organization to whom you report. Once you've reported the situation and someone else has assumed responsibility, you'd probably be wise to follow up and make sure the student is being cared for. Unfortunately, I often hear of cases where a volunteer has passed on information and then found out weeks later that nothing was being done.

It's important for us to know why, when, and how to refer students when we can't handle their pain on our own.

chapter thirteen

WHY YOU SHOULD REFER A HURTING STUDENT

We have a natural tendency to try to handle things on our own. We don't like to admit that we can't hack it or that we're carrying more than we can handle. Some of us have such a great need to be needed that we actually find ourselves feeding off the problems kids share with us. We feel good knowing that kids have trusted us with secrets that no one else knows. In some cases we've been sworn to silence (see the section at the end of this chapter on how to handle confidentiality), and asking for help feels like a violation of a commitment we've made.

It's not always easy to know what to do, but consider these good reasons why you might want to refer a student or ask someone for help.

TO ENSURE YOUR STUDENTS GET THE BEST POSSIBLE HELP

No one can offer expertise on every situation that comes along. Some of the problems kids share with us are out of our league. If we really want them to find true hope and healing, we may have no choice but to involve others in the process.

Problems often have multiple facets—relational, emotional, psychological, spiritual, physiological, cognitive, and so on—and a holistic approach may be the wisest. You might feel comfortable dealing with the spiritual side of a problem but have no idea how to handle the physiological or emotional piece. Telling a kid who cuts himself that his body is the temple of God or telling an anorexic she really ought to start eating doesn't provide the full extent of what they need.

We can actually harm students when we fail to give them the most comprehensive help possible. It's important to not allow our pride or independence to get in the way of providing students with all the support they need. Be sure you develop working relationships with the people in your community who have expertise in dealing with the specific issues you find yourself facing with the kids you care about.

TO PREVENT BURNOUT AND IMBALANCE

Each of us can handle only so much. Helping hurting kids can take a huge amount of time and emotional energy. The stories we hear from students are complex, and kids' needs are urgent. When we base our time management decisions on the depth of hurt we see around us, we can quickly start to drown in the mess. There will always be more hurting kids than we have the time to help. Telling a teenager in pain that we don't have the time he needs from us is hard, but it may be the most important skill to learn if we hope to have an ongoing ministry. Lifeguards often jump into dangerous situations, but they are trained to do so in a way that ensures their own safety—because it's pointless to have two people go down.

Burnout is inevitable when we try to give away something we don't have. Think about your work with students as being analogous to breathing—we inhale so we can exhale. Nourishing and enjoyable relationships with friends and family are like breathing in—they equip us so we can give. Without appropriate give and take in our lives, we'll find ourselves running on empty pretty quickly. I suggest that you allow yourself a bit of margin in this area. Don't push yourself to the absolute limit when it comes to the number of kids you get involved with. Leave a bit of room in your schedule for the occasional emergency or unforeseen crisis, and refer those students that you legitimately don't have time for right now. This may require you to trust God in some deep ways. Remember: There's only one Savior—and it's not you.

TO PROTECT YOURSELF LEGALLY

As youth workers we are part of a larger protective network for kids and must take our role seriously. We must understand the legal implications of working with minors, and we may need to refer specific situations to government social agencies or the police. Everyone who cares for children or adolescents has a moral responsibility to know what his legal responsibilities are.

As a general, nationwide rule of thumb: If you suspect any form of abuse is going on in the life of one of your students, you must report it. Failure to report can result in charges against you. This is not meant to be alarming or create undue fear. In most cases the organization you work for will have policies in place to handle these situations. (If it doesn't, I suggest you encourage your organization to put something in place as soon as possible.) These policies will be based on your local ordinances and bylaws, and the leaders in your organization will typically enforce the policies.

If you're not sure about the specific rules and procedures in your community, I offer these suggestions to help you find out.

- Call the local office of Health and Human Services or your regional child protection agency. It will have policy statements, brochures, or Web sites you can visit with instructions regarding the who, when, and how of reporting your concerns.

- Check with a guidance counselor or principal at a local school. They'll be well versed in the latest laws and their application in your community.

- Ask the local police. If they don't have the information, they'll be able to get it for you or tell you where to find it.

By the way, learn this information BEFORE you find yourself in the middle of a crisis. Learning to swim after you've fallen into deep water is pointless. Additionally, when you make contact with the police or child protection agencies to pick up some information, try to establish a bit of a relationship with them. Then should you need to work with them again in the future, you'll feel as though you're working with colleagues.

TO KEEP OTHERS FROM HARM

When kids share about incidents of abuse, bullying, or criminal activity, we must realize that the person hurting them may very well be hurting others, too. We're obligated to do all we can to ensure that other kids aren't left vulnerable. When you involve a professional who specializes in these areas, she'll know if the perpetrator might be putting someone else at risk and will take the necessary steps to protect others. Even reporting an incident to your supervisor might tip her off to a pattern because of other reports she has received.

In the case of behaviors that typically have multiple victims—such as drug dealing, bullying, sexual abuse, and so on—many other kids could be affected if the perpetrator isn't stopped. Teenagers will often assume that someone's behavior only impacts them, but sadly, there are often multiple victims, and we must do all we can to stop the harm immediately.

chapter fourteen

WHEN YOU SHOULD REFER A HURTING STUDENT

Deciding when to involve someone else in the helping process is often difficult. After all, the students trusted you with their stories. That trust makes you feel honored, so you may feel reluctant to invite someone else to join you in your efforts to help. However, in some circumstances it would be advisable to ask for help—especially if you're new to youth ministry or if you work as a volunteer. Don't rigidly apply each item in the following list. Each situation differs. In most cases you'll need to use your own wisdom and discernment to make the call, but here are some factors that should prompt you to seriously consider referring someone.

WHEN THERE'S A VIOLATION OF THE LAW

Obviously, violations of the law represent a broad range of possibilities, so use a measure of discernment here. I'm not suggesting that you refer or report every time a kid speeds, buys cigarettes underage, or trespasses on private property; but sometimes the situation will clearly call for the input of someone who is a level up in your organization. For example, you should report to your supervisor all cases that involve felony offenses—if only for awareness and to protect yourself from mishandling something. If you're in doubt, begin by presenting the circumstances to someone you trust (without divulging names) and get his advice on whether or not you should report the situation. These cases are always difficult because they may involve some unpleasant outcomes for the student, who may not understand your responsibility to take action.

WHEN THERE'S A MEDICAL OR PHYSIOLOGICAL CONCERN

The adolescent body is a complex machine in the midst of change and growth. A lot of the emotional, behavioral, and relational issues kids face could have physiological components. You may be dealing with a teenager who is already under the care of a physician or is taking a prescription of some sort. But in many cases, you must discern whether a problem might have a physiological connection. Eating disorders, depression, some forms of anxiety, many addictive behaviors, sexual problems, and a variety of other common adolescent issues need the input of a doctor.

As a teenager's confidante, you have a responsibility to ensure the best care possible. Don't put yourself in a position where someone could suggest you were negligent. Encourage teenagers to talk to their family physician about any issue you feel they need to address at that level. Err on the side of caution. If you believe a doctor should be involved, insist on it. Just be aware that doctors won't be able to discuss their medical findings with you unless appropriate disclosure documents have been signed.

WHEN A STUDENT TALKS ABOUT OR ATTEMPTS SUICIDE

Few circumstances leave us feeling more out of our depth than the hopelessness of a suicidal teenager. Adolescent suicide is a very real issue for kids today. It remains one of the top killers of young people. The topic of suicide is addressed in more detail later in this book, but you should know that when you're dealing with hints of suicide, suicide notes, threats, or attempts, you would be irresponsible not to involve someone else. These teenagers typically need close monitoring—a job that will probably include the other people in their lives. When kids start talking about suicide, invite help and work cooperatively. This is another situation in which kids may feel abandoned if we don't stay involved with them—even when we've referred them to someone who may be better equipped to deal with the urgent needs that a suicide threat involves.

WHEN YOU'RE BEING LIED TO (OR THINK YOU ARE)

A girl once told me a story that tore at my sensitive heart. It was a messy tale of extreme sexual abuse and an untimely pregnancy that was aborted—and the girl's dad was her abuser. He has terminal cancer now, she told me, with only a few months to live. So she didn't want to destroy her mother's life by accusing her dad in his final days. I just didn't know what to do. Some of the details of her story didn't line up; but she seemed so traumatized, I could understand how they wouldn't.

I decided to share the story with a fellow pastor in our community who did a lot of counseling. Within 30 seconds of my sharing the particulars (anonymously), he interrupted and finished the story for me—with all its sordid details. "She's a compulsive liar," he told me. "You're just one more on a whole list of people she's tried to sucker with that yarn." I was so glad I'd talked to someone who was experienced and well positioned to save me from an overreaction. Obviously, the girl had deep needs and required some serious intervention, but as long as each of her helpers tried working with her alone, that wasn't going to happen.

Ask God to give you wisdom to discern truth from lies, and when a story seems off-kilter, invite someone who is objective and trustworthy to hear the story and help you decide what the next steps ought to be.

WHEN YOU HEAR ABOUT ABUSE

This one is pretty straightforward. When we hear about kids being abused, we call for help. We're legally required to report even suspicions of abuse. The idea is to protect others from harm and to address the often-serious outcomes in the life of the victim. Guidelines for reporting abuse are covered in chapter 13, but unless you have specific training in dealing with victims of abuse or sexual assault, it's essential to involve someone else. The dynamics of abuse often express themselves in some complex ways and require a depth of intervention that most of us can't provide. The statistics on frequency of sexual abuse are grim, and the numbers seem to be growing. Because of the deep sense of personal shame and betrayal that's associated with abuse, you need to continue your support even after you've referred the student to someone else. And sexual abuse does not impact girls alone. Plenty of guys live with the pain of abuse as well, and we need to offer them a safe place to share their stories and receive help.

WHEN THERE'S AN OPPOSITE-GENDER CONCERN

Think through gender-based helping issues from at least two angles. The first is fairly straightforward. As we work with students, we'll realize that persons of our opposite gender can best handle certain situations. For example, a girl might benefit from the counsel of a mature woman, and if you're a man, referring the girl to a woman who could meet her needs would be appropriate—and vice versa of course. This is one reason I suggest an intentional gender mix on a youth ministry team.

Another issue, however, can be a little more daunting to sort through. The whole guy/girl thing comes with its own set of relational, moral, and ethical dilemmas for adults who work with teenagers. Our sexuality is at the very core of our identities, and we always have the potential to get into trouble. Remaining morally pure in all our interactions with students is absolutely critical. When a relationship begins to feel as if it compromises that commitment to purity, we must immediately step away. Either you or a student may instigate "chemistry." Either way, as adults we have the responsibility to remove ourselves from inappropriate continuations of those relationships. We can easily rationalize prolonging a liaison that provides us with improper emotional pleasure or persuade ourselves that it won't go any further. Sadly, many well-meaning youth workers can no longer work with kids because they believed the same things and found out they were wrong.

Here are a few warning signs that your connection with a student may be moving in an unhealthy direction—

- You have sexual thoughts or relational fantasies about her.

- You're jealous when you see him spending time with a fellow youth worker—especially if they're deepening their relationship.

- You look for excuses to be together as often as possible, and you look forward to your meetings because of how you feel when you are with her.

- Someone who cares about you—a spouse, a fellow youth worker, or even one of the other kids in your group—expresses concern about your relationship.

- You find yourself flirting with him and enjoying the power it gives you.

- You often feel self-conscious about how she sees you and find yourself hoping that you're making a good impression.

- You find yourself probing for information that is titillating or sexually explicit under the guise of "counseling" him.

- You rationalize your guilt feelings about any of the above, telling yourself it's no big deal and nothing wrong could possibly happen between you.

Just be cautious. I'm not trying to create a sense of paranoia, and I understand what it means to care deeply about the kids we work with. But I have seen the damage and relational devastation that occurs when adults aren't vigilant in this area.

And one more point—you must carefully choose your words when explaining your decision to end an unhealthy relationship with a student. As a general rule of thumb, the less you say, the better. This is a whole different deal than breaking up with someone your own age. Detailed explanations will only dig a deeper hole. The best approach, of course, is to guard your relationships with students so they don't stray anywhere near inappropriate behavior or feelings in the first place. But if a relationship starts to slide out of control, you must take decisive steps to ensure that no further harm is done. There will be damage—it's likely the kid won't understand. Unfortunately, that's what happens when we don't carefully guard our relationships.

Most importantly, don't leave a student without help. This discussion is about referring a student—not abandoning her. If you need to step away from a student for the reasons we've discussed, please ensure that someone else gets involved in her life.

WHEN ONE STUDENT TAKES UP MOST OF YOUR TIME

Helping hurting adolescents is always time-consuming. Most of us work with a group of students, so we have responsibility for more than one kid. Understandably, at any given time one student may need more help than the others. This is the natural rhythm of working with young people. Unfortunately when we're providing intensive care for one student, we may have limited amounts of emotional energy left over to care for the others. Managing this tension is one of the biggest challenges we face when we make ourselves available to help kids at a deeper level.

Of course we want kids to know we're willing to give them the time they need, but we can't afford to have one student hold us hostage with demands that drain us and rob us of the opportunity to be available to others. Relationships are often time-consuming because we're not sure what we're doing. Instead of helping the student move forward toward a resolution of his problems, we just spin our wheels together.

Address this problem by gently telling the student you're unable to offer him what he needs over the long haul. Kids need to know that we're not abandoning them, but we want to involve someone who will be more accessible to them. Be very careful not to communicate this in an accusing way. Instead of using "you" language, frame your offer to help them find long-term support in "I" terms. Rather than saying, "You just need more time than I have to give," you might say, "I feel as if I can't offer you what you need. I care about seeing you work through this problem, so I'd like to find you a mentor or counselor."

Some youth workers have a policy that they'll meet with a student three or four times, but if it becomes obvious that the issue needs further attention, the youth worker will refer the student to someone who can give him long-term care. The best way to deal with this: Make sure there are plenty of leaders available to your students—a ratio of one adult to five or six teenagers is usually about right.

WHEN YOU JUST DON'T KNOW WHAT TO DO

Don't be ashamed to admit when you feel you can't handle a problem on your own. Working with kids in pain leaves us feeling out of our depth more often than not. Frankly, this is the most common reason I refer kids I work with. Even professional therapists will refer their clients to someone with specialized training or specific psychological expertise. The problems kids share with us can be complicated and deeply rooted. In fact, a story that sounds fairly ordinary at first often becomes more and more complicated as it develops. It's a bit like peeling an onion, with each exposed layer revealing a deeper issue that needs processing. Typically kids will tell their stories this way to test our commitment to them. As their trust in us grows, so does the level of honesty about what's really going on. At some point we realize the problem has become more than we're able or willing to tackle.

Most of us aren't trained to handle the complex issues that kids deal with. This means that we frequently have to face our own inadequacies. When we know we're out of our depth, perhaps the worst thing we can do is pretend we know what we're doing. Learning as we go is part of the process, but making up answers or acting as if we have expertise we lack is wrong. When you're out of your depth, refer the student to someone more experienced and qualified to deal with the situation.

Be prepared—gather phone numbers, e-mail addresses, and other access information for people who can help. Become familiar with the counseling centers in your community and know their areas of specialty. Know who the mental health professionals are and how to connect needy kids with them. Have a working relationship with at least one medical doctor you trust. You can refer kids to him as a starting point. (And most doctors are well connected to the other types of helping resources in their community.)

Just remember: Referral doesn't mean abandonment. We must intentionally stay involved with a student who has come to us for help, even though we've passed her on to someone better equipped to help her work through those deeper issues.

chapter fifteen

HOW YOU SHOULD REFER A HURTING STUDENT

Keep a few important things in mind when you think about how to refer and report. First of all, openly and honestly refer kids. Don't be ashamed to tell a student you feel unqualified to offer the kind of help he needs. Let him know that you'll continue to be available to him, but you know someone (or are willing to find someone) who can offer him more help at this time. If it involves an issue that requires you to report to someone, be honest and up front about that. Tell him you're in a tough situation, and you have no choice but to involve someone else. Most kids know that certain stories can't stay secret forever.

Once you've let a student know that you plan to involve someone else, give her a choice as to how she'd like to see that come about. Whether this is a simple referral or a legally required report, I usually give kids three options:

- "You can take care of it on your own" (i.e., find a counselor, go to the doctor, file a report with the police or a child protection agency). Make sure you add that this needs to happen immediately and the student should let you know whom she talked to so you can follow up.

- "I can do it for you." (e.g., "I'll call a counselor"; "I'll make an appointment with a doctor for you"; or "I'll call the people I need to report this to and tell them what I know").

- "We can do this together." (e.g., "I'll go with you to your first counseling appointment to support you and so it won't feel so scary" or "We'll go to social services together, and I'll tell them what you've told me. You'll be right there to hear everything that's going on.")

My experience has been that most kids opt for the third choice. They already trust you, and having you there while they make the transition to a whole new level of risk can be a comfort to them.

section five

TACKLING THE TOUGH STUFF—10 TOPICS YOU NEED TO UNDERSTAND

When we work with hurting kids, we'll need to familiarize ourselves with a number of recurring themes. While each student's life story is unique, their stories frequently revolve around a short list of issues that show up over and over again. As you become a person whom teenagers trust, you may very well encounter some of the following issues. These topics are far more complex than this brief treatment would indicate, but the purpose of this section is to give you a snapshot of these common problem areas, a starting point for helping kids, and a short list of places to look for additional information.

chapter sixteen

EATING DISORDERS

HERE'S THE DEAL

Eating disorders are abnormal, unhealthy, and harmful patterns people choose as a way of dealing with deeper issues of pain in their lives. While eating disorders may begin with a preoccupation with food and weight, they're about much more than food. People with eating disorders often use food and the control over their appetites in an attempt to compensate for feelings and emotions that might otherwise seem overwhelming. The majority of people with eating disorders are adolescent and young adult females, but an increasing number of males suffer from this problem as well. The two types of eating disorders you are most likely to encounter are anorexia and bulimia.

Anorexia nervosa

Anorexia nervosa is a serious, potentially life-threatening eating disorder characterized by self-starvation and excessive weight loss. People with anorexia have an intense fear of becoming obese and distorted perceptions of their own bodies. They always claim to "feel fat" even when they are obviously underweight.

Bulimia nervosa

Bulimia nervosa is a serious, potentially life-threatening eating disorder characterized by a cycle of binging (eating excessive amounts of food) and then purging (getting rid of it) through self-induced vomiting, laxative abuse, fasting, or excessive exercise. You may find it difficult to detect bulimia because a typical bulimic's body weight is relatively normal.

STATISTICALLY SPEAKING

According to the National Association of Anorexia Nervosa and Associated Disorders—

- Eating disorders are the third most common chronic illness among females under the age of 25.

- The vast majority of women with anorexia are high achievers between the ages of 14 and 25.

- 60 percent of sixth-grade girls are now or have been on diets.

- 43 percent of eating disorders begin between the ages of 16 and 20, 33 percent between 11 and 15, 14 percent over the age of 20, and 10 percent under the age of 10.

- 90-95 percent of anorexia nervosa sufferers are female, but more guys are starting to be affected as well.

- Between 5 and 20 percent of individuals struggling with anorexia nervosa will die. The probability of death increases within that range, depending on how long a person has the condition.

- Approximately 80 percent of bulimia nervosa patients are female.

DID YOU KNOW?

- Anorexia nervosa has one of the highest death rates of any mental illness. When anorexia is fatal, the cause of death is usually a heart attack brought on by electrolytic imbalances, rather than simple malnutrition.

- Anorexia interrupts a girl's menstrual cycle, often stopping it completely.

- Recovery from bulimia can take a long time—an average of six years, including starts, stops, and slides backward.

- Adolescents often teach each other how to binge and purge and mutually enforce each other's actions.

- Although the large majority of eating disorder sufferers are female, approximately five percent of the general male population suffers from eating disorders of some kind.

- Among women who have bulimia nervosa, about 70 percent are normal weight, 15 percent are underweight, and the other 15 percent are overweight.

Many people struggle with an eating disorder for years without anyone noticing. But learning about eating disorders can help people to detect the warning signs that someone may be struggling with this. The earlier in the disease a person receives help, the higher her chances of overcoming it.

WHERE TO START

- Many people with eating disorders have low self-esteem, feel inadequate, or feel a lack of control. Show them that you care about them as unique and will accept them apart from their achievements, successes, and performance.

- Avoid giving simple solutions. Don't force-feed a sufferer or endlessly talk about food. Eating disorders often have deep and complex psychological roots.

- Avoid placing shame, blame, or guilt on the person for struggling with eating.

- Explore their feelings to discover some of the underlying issues that may have led them to develop the eating disorder.

- Encourage the teenager's initiative, independence, autonomy, and her ability to choose.

- Do not put down the eating-disordered teenager by comparing her to more "successful" siblings or friends.

- Eating disorders ALWAYS require professional intervention. Require a medical examination and refer the person to a qualified counselor.

DIGGING DEEPER

Here's a list of suggested resources to help you more fully understand eating disorders. Use these as starting points if you need to go deeper.

Recommended Reading

Diary of an Anorexic Girl by Morgan Menzie

Eating Disorders: The Facts by Suzanne Abraham and Derek Llewellyn-Jones

Eating Disorders: A Question and Answer Book about Anorexia Nervosa and Bulimia Nervosa by Ellen Erlanger

The Truth about Eating Disorders by Mark J. Kittleson, Ph.D. (general ed.) and Gerri Freid Kramer (ed.)

Surfing the Web

American Anorexia/Bulimia Association:
www.aabainc.org

Mirror-Mirror: *www.mirror-mirror.org*

National Association of Anorexia and Associated Disorders (ANAD): *www.anad.org*

National Eating Disorders Association:
www.nationaleatingdisorders.org

National Eating Disorder Information Center (NEDIC):
www.nedic.ca

Toll-Free Hotlines

ANAD Hotline: 1-847-831-3438

Bulimia/Anorexia Self-Help Hotline: 1-800-227-4785

NEDIC Hotline: 1-866-633-4220

chapter seventeen
ADOLESCENT SUICIDE

HERE'S THE DEAL

Suicide is the third leading cause of death for adolescents in North America (after accidents and homicide). Kids who struggle with suicide almost always carry with them a deep sense of hopelessness and a faulty sense of reasoning. The most common reason teenagers commit suicide is to escape the problems they're facing. They view death as the only solution to their circumstances and the only way to end the pain.

Some teenagers who commit suicide direct the act toward one or more survivors. They want to make those they leave behind suffer and feel guilty or responsible for their suicide. If this is the case, the teenager will often plan his suicide in such a way so that the person to whom the suicide is directed will find the body. Other reasons teenagers attempt suicide are to manipulate others, to gain attention or fame, to be reunited with a deceased loved one, to express love, and to avoid being a burden on those around them.

STATISTICALLY SPEAKING

According to the American Association for Suicidology—

- The adolescent suicide rate has tripled since 1970.

- Boys are three to six times more likely than girls to commit suicide, and girls are four to six times more likely than boys to attempt suicide. Boys die more often because they use more lethal methods.

- Suicide among preteens and early teens (ages 10-14) has doubled since the 1960s.

- In the U.S. in 2002, 4,010 young people (ages 15-24) committed suicide. That means that on average, a young person commits suicide every 2 hours and 11 minutes.

- For every adolescent who commits suicide, 50-100 teenagers attempt it—that's about two million suicide attempts each year.

DID YOU KNOW?

- Most adolescent suicide attempts occur at home during the after school hours.

Some warning signs that someone may be considering suicide:

- Depression and talk about feelings of hopelessness or irresolvable guilt

- A recent traumatic event (e.g., physical illness, breakup of a romance, divorce of parents, failure in school)

- Irrational outbursts

- Changes in eating or sleeping habits (either a big increase or a big decrease from the norm)

- A history of problems (suicide is usually not an impulsive act)

- A decline in performance (e.g., grades, sports, etc.)

- Talking about suicide or making a plan to do it

- Giving away their prized or valuable possessions

- Drug or alcohol abuse

- Withdrawal from social circles

- A previous suicide attempt

WHERE TO START

Be alert for signals and warning signs, especially spoken statements such as, "It just doesn't seem like there's any point in going on"; " It would be a lot simpler for everyone if I just wasn't around anymore"; or "Some days I just feel like packing it all in."

If a student is making those kinds of statements, you can ask her direct questions about her intentions: "Are you trying to tell me you're considering suicide?"

If you ever confront a direct suicide threat or sense that a kid is seriously considering suicide, the following diagnostic categories—corresponding to the letters *S, L, A,* and *P*—will help you assess the seriousness of the threat. Obviously, any threat or consideration of suicide is very serious, so never take it lightly.

S=specific: Is there a SPECIFIC suicide plan in place? "Yeah, my dad's guns and ammo are in the cabinet, and I'm doin' it Friday night out by the ravine" is more urgent than "I dunno—there are lots of ways I could do it."

L=lethal: Will the chosen method be fatal, and do you have time for intervention? For example, although both are potentially lethal, a gun represents an even greater urgency than a drug overdose, which offers a small window of opportunity in which to intervene.

A=availability: Is the chosen means of suicide immediately available? A statement such as, "I'm picking up the pills this weekend at the mall," while representing a great cause for alarm, is less urgent than, "I'm holding the gun as we speak."

P=proximity of help: Is there anyone nearby who could intervene or provide support? "I'm in my room, and my parents are downstairs watching TV" is more hopeful than "I'm at our summer cottage, and there's no one around for miles."

Remember: Kids contemplate suicide when they feel there are NO OTHER OPTIONS. Whatever you can do to create even one more option can buy some time and potentially save a life. Pray, remain calm, listen, avoid power struggles, don't "call their bluff," and hope you never need to use this information.

Consider making a written contract for life with the adolescent—this communicates to the teenager that you care about her and the importance of her life to you.

DIGGING DEEPER
Some suggested resources to help you more fully understand adolescent suicide. Use these as starting points if you need to go deeper.

Recommended Reading

Evaluating and Treating Adolescent Suicide Attempters: From Research to Practice by Anthony Spirito and James C. Overholser

One in Thirteen: The Silent Epidemic of Teen Suicide by Jessica Portner

Out of the Darkness: Teens Talk about Suicide by Marion Crook

Suicide: A Christian Response by Timothy J. Demy and Gary P. Stewart (eds.)

Teen Suicide: Just the Facts by Claire Wallerstein

Why Suicide? Answers to 200 of the Most Frequently Asked Questions about Suicide by Eric Marcus

Surfing the Web

The American Association of Suicidology:
www.suicidology.org

American Foundation for Suicide Prevention:
www.afsp.org

Suicide Awareness Voices of Education:
www.save.org

Suicide Prevention Action Network USA: *www.spanusa.org*

Youth Suicide Prevention Program: *www.yspp.org*

Toll-Free Hotlines

American Foundation for Suicide Prevention—Suicide Hotline: 1-888-333-2377

National Hopeline Network: 1-800-SUICIDE (784-2433)

National Suicide Prevention Lifeline: 1-800-273-TALK (8255)

chapter eighteen

RAPE, ACQUAINTANCE RAPE, AND SEXUAL ASSAULT

HERE'S THE DEAL

Rape can be broadly defined as any sexual act forced upon a person against her will. When the sexual act occurs in the context of a dating relationship, it is termed "date" or "acquaintance" rape. Acquaintance rape occurs when the victim knows her attacker and may or may not be romantically involved with him. Date or acquaintance rape occurs when someone is coerced into performing a sexual act with a romantic partner or an acquaintance by emotional manipulation, physical force, intimidation, or the use of drugs or alcohol. The repercussions of rape include stigma, shame, guilt, shock, confusion, hostility, post-traumatic stress disorder, and rape trauma syndrome.

STATISTICALLY SPEAKING

- According to the Justice Department, girls under 18 are victims of half the nation's rapes every year.

- 20-25 percent of college women report experiencing sexual assault as students, but most do not report it to authorities.

- For females ages 14-17, victimization rates are 10 times greater than males, with the greatest risk for sexual victimization at age 14.

- 71 percent of sexual assaults against older juveniles (between 12 and 17 years of age) and 84 percent of assaults against juveniles under 12 occur at their homes or in residences.

- 60 percent of all females who lose their virginity before age 15 say that their first sexual experience was forced.

DID YOU KNOW?

- Susan Brownmiller and Diana Russell coined the term "date rape" in a feminist study called "Against Our Will" in the mid-1970s.

- Acquaintance rape is most likely to happen to women between the ages of 15 and 19.

- Acquaintance rape is often characterized by coercion and manipulation, while forcible stranger rape is characterized by verbal threats, physical violence, and use of weapons.

- An adolescent who has experienced acquaintance rape may feel more responsible and guilty than a victim of stranger rape and may blame herself for leading the attacker on or for being drunk or high.

- An adolescent who has experienced stranger rape may have less guilt and an increased chance of seeking counseling.

- An adolescent who has experienced stranger rape may also experience more anxiety and panic in everyday situations and have trouble sleeping or eating.

- Two of the more common date rape drugs, gamma-hydroxybutyrate (GHB) and Rohypnol ("Roofies") are central nervous system depressants that become odorless and tasteless when dissolved in both alcoholic and nonalcoholic beverages. Once a person ingests one of these drugs, she becomes disoriented, confused, and may not be aware of an attack until 8-12 hours after it occurs. In an effort to reduce the incidence of drug-facilitated rape, pharmaceutical companies recently included a color additive to the drug Rohypnol. Ketamine (also known as "Special K") actually is an animal tranquilizer, for which perpetrators have been known to rob veterinary clinics.

WHERE TO START

- The best place to start is prevention. Tell the adolescent to keep dates public, always have enough money to get home, make decisions about the details of her dates, offer to pay her share (so she doesn't "owe him one"), and avoid or limit alcohol intake to avoid vulnerable situations.

- Tell the adolescent that active forms of resistance (physical struggling, screaming, trying to run away, attacking back) are the most effective ways to stop a rape.

- Be aware of the extra dangers the Internet poses. Kids can be violated through inappropriate conversations and other forms of online sexual interactions. They may feel anonymous and get in over their heads. And most importantly, if you ever hear kids talking about going to meet someone they met online, immediately step in.

- If a student in your group has been raped, you may be the first person the survivor has ever told about the assault. Your response will be important; it could set the tone for how she feels about herself and the events in the future. A caring, nonjudgmental response will help in her recovery.

Understand the reasons why teenagers don't report date rape:

- To protect the family. "Yeah, it happened to me. I can handle it, but there's no way my parents could."

- Conflicting values. "If my mom and dad knew I went to those kinds of parties where I got raped, they'd kill me. They think I'm still a virgin."

- Desire to maintain independence. "If I told them what happened to me, they'd never let me out of the house again!"

- Psychological distance. "Tell my parents? Why would I even want to talk to them?"

- Close proximity to the offender. "I've got to face this guy every day at school. If I told anyone, they'd side with him, and his friends would get after me too."

- Actively listen to and believe the adolescent. Validate her fears and pain.

DIGGING DEEPER

Some suggested resources to help you more fully understand rape and sexual assault. Use these as starting points if you need to go deeper.

Recommended Reading

The Date Rape Prevention Book by Scott Lindquist

Dating Violence: Young Women in Danger by Barrie Levy (ed.)

I Never Called It Rape by Robin Warshaw

Straight Talk about Date Rape by Susan Mufson and Rachel Kranz

Surfing the Web

Hope for Healing: *www.hopeforhealing.org*

The Rape, Abuse & Incest National Network (RAINN): *www.rainn.org*

Promote Truth (online support): www.promotetruth.org

Toll-Free Hotlines

National Sexual Assault Hotline: 1-800-656-HOPE (4673)

(Note: Your local community may also have its own rape or sexual assault hotline.)

chapter nineteen

ADOLESCENT PREGNANCY

HERE'S THE DEAL

Adolescent pregnancy interrupts the formation of the teenager's identity and the development of autonomy, which may affect the mother's relationship with the child or lead to maladaptive behaviors. According to the National Criminal Justice Reference Service, the U.S. has the highest teenage pregnancy rate of all industrialized countries. Nearly one million teenagers become pregnant each year (or 10 percent of 15-to-19-year-olds). Teenage pregnancy rates increased between 1970 and 1990 but have been declining since then. The rates are still twice as high in the U.S. when compared to other countries, and they're higher now than they were in the 1970s. But they are decreasing.

STATISTICALLY SPEAKING

According to the Youth Risk Behavior Survey (CDC, 2001)—

- In the U.S., 800,000-900,000 adolescents become pregnant each year.

- 52 percent carry their babies to term, 33 percent abort, 14 percent miscarry, and less than four percent choose adoption.

- Only one fourth of the men who impregnate girls under the age of 18 are also younger than 18 years old.

- 20 percent of teenagers who become pregnant do so within one month of their first sexual intercourse experience.

- 67 percent of teenagers suggest an increased emphasis on abstinence and birth control to decrease the rates of pregnancy.

DID YOU KNOW?

- On prime-time networks, there are eight depictions of pre-marital sex for each sex act between married couples.

- 50 percent of fathers who impregnate teenage mothers are five to six years older than their partners.

- Babies born to adolescent mothers suffer more physical problems—such as low birth weight, mental delays, blindness, deafness, mental illness, cerebral palsy, high infant mortality rates, and malnourishment—than those born to older mothers.

- These babies are also exposed to more violence, abuse, and neglect, and they're also more likely to do poorly in school.

- According to the National Criminal Justice Reference Service, sons of adolescent mothers are 2.7 times as likely to be incarcerated as sons born to older mothers.

- According to the National Campaign to Prevent Teen Pregnancy, 70 percent of prisoners in the U.S. were children of teenage mothers.

- The lack of a strong male role model is a factor in unplanned pregnancies and early sexual experience—for both guys and girls.

WHERE TO START

Do—

- Stay connected, talk to adolescents.

- Listen to them and validate their feelings surrounding the pregnancy.

- Realize that their emotions are going to be intense and extreme.

- Discuss the realities of having a baby (financial, emotional, and physical responsibilities).

- Discuss the options and consider the outcomes for the baby, the mom, the dad, and the grandparents. Be aware that all of the options have huge implications for everyone who's involved in the situation.

Do not—

- Judge the adolescent, lay blame, or make him or her feel guilty.

- Condemn the decisions they make regarding the pregnancy (provided these aren't harmful to the adolescent).

- Tell the adolescents how to feel about the pregnancy.

- Encourage the adolescents to get married.

DIGGING DEEPER

Some suggested resources to help you more fully understand adolescent pregnancy. Use these as starting points if you need to go deeper.

Recommended Reading

How to Survive Your Teen's Pregnancy: Practical Advice for a Christian Family by Linda Ellen Perry

Teen Pregnancy and Parenting by Helen Cothran (ed.)

The Youngest Parents: Teenage Pregnancy as it Shapes Lives by Robert Coles

Surfing the Web

America's Pregnancy Helpline: *www.thehelpline.org*

Healthy Teen Network (formerly the National Organization on Pregnancy, Parenting, and Prevention): *www.noappp.org*

The National Campaign to Prevent Teen Pregnancy: *www.teenpregnancy.org*

Toll-Free Hotlines

Christian Teen Helpline: 1-800-394-HOPE (4673)

Crisis Pregnancy Hotlines: 1-800-4-OPTIONS or 1-800-672-2296

National Child Abuse Hotline: 1-800-4-A-CHILD (422-4453)

chapter twenty

SUBSTANCE ABUSE

HERE'S THE DEAL

Adolescents' use and abuse of chemical substances is one of society's biggest challenges today. Adolescents choose to experiment with drugs and alcohol for many reasons—media influence being one of the biggest reasons. Movies, television shows, commercials, and popular celebrities often glamorize drinking. They give the impression that if you use drugs, then your life will be more fun and full of excitement.

Another reason is peer pressure. Many teenagers have the impression that to be cool, they have to go to parties and get drunk. Teenagers believe that if they can drink alcohol or use drugs, they'll become more popular and others will accept them. A third reason is family factors. Adolescents who come from families with a history of drug abuse are more susceptible to falling into the same lifestyle patterns.

STATISTICALLY SPEAKING

- 65 percent of teenagers who drink alcohol report that they get the alcohol from family and friends (Greater Dallas Council on Alcohol and Drug Abuse, www.gdcada.org).

- By the eighth grade, 52 percent of adolescents have consumed alcohol, 41 percent have smoked cigarettes, and 20 percent have used marijuana.

- The average age when kids first try alcohol is 11 years for boys and 13 years for girls. The average age at which Americans begin regularly drinking is 15.9 years old (National Institute on Alcohol Abuse and Alcoholism).

- Adolescent drug use is on the rise. In 1991, an average of 20.7 percent of high schoolers had used an illicit drug in the past year. By 2002, this average had increased to 31.2 percent.

DID YOU KNOW?

- Four main categories of drugs are often abused:

- Depressants (e.g., alcohol, inhalants such as glue and nail polish remover, and sedatives): These slow down nervous system activity.

- Stimulants (e.g., caffeine, nicotine, and cocaine): These increase nervous system activity and give the illusion of improving a person's emotional depression.

- Hallucinogens (e.g., marijuana and LSD): These distort the mind and cause hallucinations.

- Narcotics (e.g., morphine, codeine, and heroin): These can relieve physical pain but are highly addictive.

- The number one drug problem among youth today is alcoholism, and it's growing rapidly.

- Another factor in substance abuse is a teenager's personality. Teenagers who struggle with issues of low self-esteem, low expectations, low self-control, or high levels of adventure-seeking or high-risk behaviors are more likely to experiment with drug use.

- The statistics for heavy drug use for churched and unchurched kids are almost identical.

- In one hour of prime-time television, an average of 10-11 drinking acts (ingestion of alcohol or preparation to drink) are shown. By the time the average teenager is 18 years old, he has seen 100,000 beer commercials on television.

WHERE TO START

- Parents need to get involved in the intervention process—the earlier the better.

- Replace opportunities for drug-related behavior with health-promoting behavior (e.g., participating in sports, joining a church youth group).

- Give teenagers opportunities to contribute in meaningful ways at school, with the family, or in the community.

- Let teenagers know they can trust you for confidentiality—but let them know the limits of it. Confidentiality must be broken if you feel the drugs are endangering their health or if they're involved in the sale of drugs, which could potentially be dangerous to them or other kids.

- Use available programs (e.g., Alcoholics Anonymous, drug rehab centers).

- Teach teenagers proper methods for stress management. Many adolescents don't know how to appropriately handle the pressures in their lives and use drugs as a means of escaping or coping with the stress.

Four Things That Will Keep Kids Off Drugs—

1. Mentoring—Kids involved with a Big Brothers/Big Sisters program are 46 percent less likely to start using drugs than those kids who don't have a mentor but want one.

2. Responsibility—Young people who have goals of marriage and raising a family are less likely to abuse drugs.

3. Connection to a religious or family community—A church can serve as an extended family for adolescents and can play a parental role by protecting children from negative influences.

4. Life-skills education—A new public school program called Life Skills Training (www.lifeskillstraining.com)

teaches kids how to develop social skills and solve problems. Those skills, in turn, help them resist the pressure to do drugs.

DIGGING DEEPER

Some suggested resources to help you more fully understand drug and alcohol abuse. Use these as starting points if you need to go deeper.

Recommended Reading

Drug and Alcohol Abuse: The Authoritative Guide for Parents, Teachers, and Counselors by H. Thomas Milhorn, Jr., M.D., Ph.D.

Drug-Proof Your Kids by Stephen Arterburn and Jim Burns

Drugs and Your Kid: How to Tell if Your Child Has a Drug/Alcohol Problem and What to Do about It by Peter D. Rogers, Ph.D. and Lea Goldstein, Ph.D.

Good News for the Chemically Dependent and Those Who Love Them by Jeff VanVonderen

Illegal Drugs: A Complete Guide to Their History, Chemistry, Use and Abuse by Paul M. Gahlinger, M.D., Ph.D.

Surfing the Web

Alateen: *www.al-anon.alateen.org*

Alcoholics anonymous: *www.alcoholics-anonymous.org*

A Family Guide to Keeping Youth Mentally Healthy and Drug Free: *http://family.samhsa.gov*

National Institute on Drug Abuse: *www.drugabuse.gov*

The Partnership for a Drug-Free America: *www.drugfree.org*

Toll-Free Hotlines

Alcoholics Anonymous/Alateen: 1-888-4AL-ANON (425-2666)

The Center for Substance Abuse Treatment: 1-800-662-HELP (4357)

The National Federation of Parents for Drug-Free Youth: 1-800-554-KIDS (5437)

chapter twenty-one

GRIEF AND LOSS

HERE'S THE DEAL

One of the biggest challenges a youth worker will face is to walk with a teenager who has lost a close friend or family member. Grief is defined as deep mental anguish arising from bereavement, frustration, trouble, or difficulty. When grieving, teenagers may experience questions about who they are, how they'll survive, and their prospects for the future without the deceased, as well as acute separation distress, intense longing for the deceased, a sense of emptiness, a lack of purpose, a strong sense of being detached from others, and numbness. According to Earl Grollman, in his book *Living When a Young Friend Commits Suicide*, adolescents are also the first developmental group to encounter the full range of cross-generational deaths.

STATISTICALLY SPEAKING

According to the Child Bereavement Study conducted by the U.S. Bureau of the Census in 2001—

- One in 20 children or adolescents experiences the loss of a parent before the age of 18.

- Boys act out through anger and aggression more than girls do.

- Boys are more prone to learning and concentration difficulties in the first year after a loss.

- Boys who lose a parent show more depression and anxiety than do girls who lose a parent.

- Girls talk and cry more and show more anxiety than guys do.

- Girls show more concern over their own health and the health and safety of others than boys do.

- Girls remain more attached to the person who died than boys do.

- Girls who lose a sibling show more anxiety, depression, and attention difficulties than boys do.

In a 1993 survey conducted by the YWCA of Indianapolis at the Indiana Juvenile Correctional Facility—

- 141 of 150 female offenders had experienced at least one painful loss prior to incarceration.

- A 2003 update of the survey found that 99 percent of those surveyed had experienced multiple losses prior to incarceration.

- 61 percent admitted to using drugs or alcohol, and 35 percent engaged in self-injury to cope with the loss.

DID YOU KNOW?

- The stages of grief in adolescence may include denial, anger, bargaining, guilt or depression, and acceptance—just like adults.

- Adolescent emotions involved in grief and loss may include sadness, shock, denial, anger, fear, guilt, depression, fatigue, anxiety, and thoughts of suicide.

- Teenagers may also feel rejected if the loss involved a severed relationship with a parent or other significant person, a family breakdown, or a suicide.

WHERE TO START

Do—

- Honestly answer their questions.

- Address the adolescent's anxiety and worry.

- Offer multiple ways to express grief, including drawing, poetry, writing letters or stories, creating memory books, planting trees, or raising funds to support a worthy cause.

- Challenge the guilt and self-blame that's present.

- Allow the adolescent to choose how to remember the person he's lost.

- Allow the adolescent to talk about the deceased.

- Give the adolescent time and space to talk at his own pace and comfort level.

- Validate the feelings that accompany grief and loss.

- Provide continuity and predictability in the environment (with routines and boundaries).

- Explore spiritual implications or troubles, if appropriate.

- Reassure the adolescent that his grief is unique and can be uniquely expressed.

- Encourage the adolescent to maintain an attachment to the deceased (visit the grave, pray, keep a possession that once belonged to the deceased).

- Talk to the adolescent's peers and friends and let them know their buddy needs peer support and someone his own age to talk to.

- Go to funerals and visitations, if appropriate, to show support.

- Reassure the adolescent that the person's death was not his fault, particularly in the case of suicide.

- Let the adolescent know that nothing will immediately take his grief and pain away.

- Frequently reassure the adolescent.

- Model healthy grieving: Talk about the loss and share memories with the student.

Don't—

- Say, "I know how you feel."

- Encourage the adolescent to "get over it."

- Give advice.

- Minimize the loss or the adolescent's pain, no matter how trivial you think it is.

- Encourage cheerfulness.

- Avoid speaking of the deceased or using his or her name in conversation.

- Avoid acknowledging that a death or loss has occurred.

- Tell the adolescent there are right and wrong ways to experience grief.

- Accept joking about the loss or the death if it's a defensive coping mechanism.

Things to be aware of—

- Mourning rituals can be extremely helpful.

- Online counseling and Internet bereavement discussion groups are available for adolescents who aren't comfortable talking face-to-face with a counselor or adult (http://kidsaid.com).

- Be sensitive to and honest about losses that involve suicide, particularly parental suicide.

- Try to involve the family as much as possible.

- Group therapy may be successful for adolescents because they're developing more independence from the family and identifying with their peer group.

- Watch for risky behaviors such as sexual promiscuity, self-harm, drug or alcohol abuse, or suicidal thoughts in response to the loss.

- Expect the recurrence of grief.

DIGGING DEEPER

Some suggested resources to help you more fully understand grieving kids. Use these as starting points if you need to go deeper.

Recommended Reading

The Grieving Teen: A Guide for Teenagers and Their Friends by Helen Fitzgerald

Guiding Your Child through Grief by Mary Ann Emswiler, M.A., M.P.S., and James P. Emswiler, M.A., M.Ed.

Living When a Young Friend Commits Suicide or Even Starts Talking about It by Earl Grollman and Max Malikow

Surfing the Web

American Hospice Foundation: *www.americanhospice.org*

The Grief Recovery Institute: *www.grief.net*

KIDSAID (by GriefNet): *http://kidsaid.com*

Teen Grief: *www.newhope-grief.org/teengrief*

Toll-Free Hotlines

Girls & Boys Town National Hotline USA: 1-800-448-3000

National Youth Crisis Hotline: 1-800-442-HOPE (4673)

chapter twenty-two

SELF-INJURY

HERE'S THE DEAL

Self-injury or self-mutilation is the act of physically hurting yourself without the intent of committing suicide. It's attempting to alter your mood state by inflicting physical harm serious enough to cause tissue damage to your body. Self-mutilation can take the form of cutting, burning, hitting, hair pulling, scratching, and so on. Self-injury is a method of coping during an emotionally difficult time. It helps some people feel better, at least temporarily, because they find a physical way to express and release the tension, pain, and pent-up feelings they're holding inside. For some people, hurting themselves produces chemical changes in their bodies that make them feel happier and more relaxed.

STATISTICALLY SPEAKING

- 65 percent of self-injuring women have been sexually or physically abused or have at least one alcoholic parent.

- Approximately one percent of the U.S. population uses physical self-injury to deal with overwhelming feelings or situations.

- 90 percent of self-injurers begin as teenagers.

- In one study done with university students, one in eight (12 percent) people had deliberately cut, burned, or similarly harmed themselves at least once in their lives.

- Self-injury occurs at nearly 30 times the rate of suicide attempts and 140 times the rate of "successful" suicides.

- The typical self-injurer is a white woman in her mid 20s who began hurting herself at age 14 and has done so about 50 times since then.

DID YOU KNOW?

- There are two common characteristics among people who cut: a feeling of mental disintegration or an inability to think, and a rage that cannot be expressed or even consciously perceived but is typically directed toward a powerful figures in their lives. These experiences become unbearable and must be drowned out by some immediate method.

- Most self-injurers come from middle- or upper middle-class backgrounds, are well educated, and sometimes have eating disorders as well.

- Emotionally, self-injurers generally feel inferior, are oversensitive to rejection, have difficulty expressing their anger, and have trouble coping with the problems of life.

WHERE TO START

- Self-injurers often feel invisible—as if they don't matter to anyone. So they need reassurance that they do matter. We must help them to feel visible again.

- They need to establish strong, close relationships with people they trust.

- Don't avoid or ignore the fact that they injure themselves. Address it, talk about it, and offer to help them—they need and want this, so don't be afraid. We don't have to know the perfect words to say. Just be there and love them.

- They need to understand why they hurt themselves and what circumstances cause them to want to act out this way.

- Self-injurers need to understand their own patterns of self-harm. Help them recognize and avoid their triggers.

- Help them find new, healthy ways to cope with stress.

DIGGING DEEPER

Some suggested resources to help you understand cutters and other self-injurers more fully. Use these as starting points if you need to go deeper.

Recommended Reading

A Bright Red Scream: Self-Mutilation and the Language of Pain by Marilee Strong

Coping With Self-Mutilation: A Helping Book for Teens Who Hurt Themselves by Alicia Clarke

Cutting the Pain Away: Understanding Self-Mutilation by Ann Holmes, Carol C. Nadelson, M.D. (ed.), and Claire E. Reinburg (ed.)

The Scarred Soul: Understanding and Ending Self-Inflicted Violence by Tracy Alderman, Ph.D.

Secret Scars: Uncovering and Understanding the Addiction of Self-Injury by V.J. Turner

Surfing the Web

The National Self-Harm Network: *www.nshn.co.uk*

Self-Injury, Abuse & Trauma Resource Directory: *www.self-injury-abuse-trauma-directory.info*

Self-Injury & Related Issues: *www.siari.co.uk*

Self-Injury Information and Support: *www.psyke.org*

Self-Injury Support: *www.palace.net/~llama/psych/injury.html*

Young People & Self-Harm: *www.selfharm.org.uk*

Toll-Free Hotlines

S.A.F.E. (Self-Abuse Finally Ends) Alternatives: 1-800-DON'T-CUT (366-8288)

chapter twenty-three

FAMILY BREAKDOWN

HERE'S THE DEAL

The family is meant to be a safe place of nurture and intimacy. Teenagers who live in chaotic family situations are substantially more vulnerable to maladaptive and destructive coping mechanisms. When we work with teenagers, we must understand them in the context of their primary family units. Divorce tears family units apart, and remarriage creates blended family units that teenagers often find to be more uncomfortable than the original family unit—in spite of its unhealthy state. When the family breaks down, no one wins. Allow the church to become "family" for kids whose families aren't functioning.

STATISTICALLY SPEAKING

- Since 1970, at least one million children each year have watched their parents divorce.
- 40 percent of all married adults in the 1990s had already been divorced.
- 80 percent of divorces occur during the first nine years of marriage.

Children of divorce—

- are more aggressive toward parents and teachers.
- experience more depression and other psychological problems.
- experience more learning difficulties and suffer more problems with peers.

- are two to three times more likely to be referred for psychological help at school.

- have earlier sexual activity.

- have more children born out of wedlock.

- experience less happiness in marriage and (when they do marry) divorce more often.

- generally feel lonelier.

- are more likely to cohabitate than marry someone, for fear of divorce.

DID YOU KNOW?

- Many children believe they're the cause of the divorce and blame themselves for it.

- Young girls can experience the emotional loss of their father as personal rejection. And if fathers continue their lack of involvement in their children's lives, girls may experience this withdrawal as an ongoing rejection. Many girls feel they've been rejected because they're not pretty enough, affectionate enough, athletic enough, or smart enough to please their fathers and engage them in regular, frequent contact.

- The marital bond and the parent-child relationship are closely linked—when the marriage works, the couple is content and the parents' love and appreciation for each other nourishes and rewards the parent-child relationship.

- The major impact of divorce does not occur during childhood or adolescence but arises in adulthood when serious romantic relationships become more important.

WHERE TO START

- Children of divorce need more education about how to have healthy relationships with the opposite sex, what to look for in prospective spouses, and how a healthy family should function—since they probably haven't had this modeled for them.

- Encourage kids to talk candidly with their parents about the divorce, ask questions, and have an open dialogue, if it's safe to do so.

- Encourage children of divorce to delay marriage or a serious commitment until they learn more about themselves and what they want in a partner.

- Encourage them to observe other relationships and see what works and what they like about them.

- Openly talk about relationships with these kids and help them struggle through their questions.

- Many children are aware of their parents' distress during a divorce and try to rescue their parents. We need to ensure kids of divorce that their parents can look out for themselves. Encourage kids to be children while they can and just have fun.

- Encourage parents to spend more time with their children after the divorce (and on through their adolescent years), giving the kids extra support and encouragement.

DIGGING DEEPER

Some suggested resources to help you more fully understand teenagers with divorced parents. Use these as starting points if you need to go deeper.

Recommended Reading

The Unexpected Legacy of Divorce by Judith S. Wallerstein, Julia M. Lewis, and Sandra Blakeslee

Surfing the Web

Christian Youth Interactive Revival: *www.byfaith.co.uk/pauldivorce.htm*

Divorce Kids—A Child's Perspective: *http://www.divorce-kids.com/*

Teens Health: *http://kidshealth.org/teen/your_mind/ families/divorce.html*

Toll-Free Hotlines

National Domestic Violence Hotline (NDVH): 1-800-799-7233

(The name of the organization seems narrower in scope than the services the NDVH actually provides—help for kids in all kinds of family trouble.)

chapter twenty·four
PORNOGRAPHY AND SEXUAL ADDICTIONS

HERE'S THE DEAL

Sexual addiction is a compulsive set of sexually motivated behaviors marked by secrecy, abusive practices (to self or others), use of sexual behaviors to alter moods, and sex outside of a caring, committed relationship. Most sex addicts trace the beginnings of their addictions back to pornography use. Today the widespread dissemination of pornography is reaching our nation's teenagers, and like users of illicit drugs, many teenagers have become hooked. Therefore, we're experiencing an alarming increase in the numbers of young people who struggle with sex addiction earlier in life.

STATISTICALLY SPEAKING

- Pornography has grown into a $10 billion business—that's more than the NFL, NBA, and Major League Baseball combined.

- Hollywood releases 11,000 adult movies each year—more than 20 times the rate of mainstream movie production.

- In 1998, 14 million pages of pornography were identified online. By 2003, this number had grown to 260 million—a 20-fold increase in only five years.

- In a study of 600 Americans, junior high school age and above, 91 percent of males and 82 percent of females said they'd been exposed to X-rated, hard-core pornography.

- Among high schoolers, 31 percent of the males and 18 percent of the females admitted doing some of the things they'd seen in pornography within a few days after exposure.

- 89 percent of juvenile sex offenders—typically males (90 percent) between the ages of 13 and 17—say they use sexually explicit materials.

DID YOU KNOW?

Most sexual addicts pass through five stages:

- Early exposure, usually through pornography or sexual abuse.

- Addiction. Like a drug, sexually stimulating material keeps the addict coming back for more.

- Escalation. The addict craves more and more explicit, violent, or deviant material.

- Desensitization. The addict becomes numb and grows desperate to feel the same thrill again but can't find it.

- Acting out sexually. The addict moves on to the real world to experience his sexual high through voyeurism, exhibitionism, rape, use of prostitutes, or abuse of others.

Porn is physiologically addictive. When people view pornography, their bodies release the adrenal hormone epinephrine, which locks memories into the brain. (This explains why men can remember pornographic images they saw years earlier.) In response to pleasure, chemicals called "opioids" are released by the nerve endings, reinforcing the body's desire to repeat the process.

WHERE TO START

There are seven crucial ingredients in a recovery from sexual addiction—

1. Acknowledgment and recognition of a serious problem.

2. Counseling—individual or group therapy that challenges not just the behaviors but also the underlying false core beliefs the addict has about himself.

3. Reaching out for the power of God.

4. Accountability—at least one other individual with whom the addict can be completely honest about his sexual behavior and viewing habits.

5. Lifestyle changes—limiting or removing Internet access, placing the computer in a public place, destroying or deleting pornography, changing friends, and finding new habits and activities.

6. Recognizing and dealing with other addictions that may be intertwined with sexual addiction (drug abuse, alcoholism, gambling).

7. Ongoing maintenance and accountability.

DIGGING DEEPER

Some suggested resources to help you more fully understand the sexual issues kids face. Use these as starting points if you need to go deeper.

Recommended Reading

Focus on the Family's Dare to Dig Deeper Booklet: Toxic Porn by Gene McConnell and Keith Campbell

Every Young Man's Battle: Strategies for Victory in the Real World of Sexual Temptation by Stephen Arterburn and Fred Stoeker, with Mike Yorkey

In the Shadows of the Net: Breaking Free of Compulsive Online Sexual Behavior by Patrick Carnes, Ph.D.; David L. Delmonico, Ph.D.; Elizabeth Griffin, M.A.; with Joseph M. Moriarty

Surfing the Web

National Council on Sexual Addiction Problems: *www.ncsac.org*

Net Accountability: *www.netaccountability.com*

Pure Online: *www.pureonline.com*

XXXchurch: *www.xxxchurch.com*

Toll-Free Hotlines

Overcomers Outreach: 1-800-310-3001

chapter twenty-five

ADOLESCENT DEPRESSION

HERE'S THE DEAL

Everybody feels down or blue at some point in time, especially teenagers. But sometimes the blues cross the line into serious depression. Depression comes in various types and has a variety of causes. Endogenous depression is caused by biological factors: hormones, brain chemistry, or infection. Reactive depression comes as the result of a real or imagined loss and usually lasts a few months. Neurotic depression is a long-term depression that develops from the attempt to escape from other emotions. Adolescents most often experience reactive depression. Regardless of the type, depressive disorders always include either sad or irritable moods or a loss of interest in life.

STATISTICALLY SPEAKING

- In children and adolescents, a depressive episode lasts an average of seven to nine months. Most young people with depression experience a recurrence.

- 20-40 percent of depressed young people relapse within two years, and 70 percent will relapse by adulthood.

- 20-40 percent of adolescents with depression eventually develop bipolar disorder.

- Depression increases the risk of suicide 12-fold in teenagers.

- 20 percent of adolescents in the general population have emotional problems.

- A third of adolescents attending psychiatric clinics suffer from depression.
- 20-25 percent of boys report having depressed moods.
- 25-40 percent of girls report having depressed moods.

DID YOU KNOW?

- After age 15, depression is twice as common in girls and women as in boys and men.
- Depression is called "the common cold of mental illness."
- Throughout history, depression has been treated with remedies such as whipping, bloodletting, exorcism, and soothing baths. Antidepressant medication was developed in the 1960s, and today there are more than 16 varieties of antidepressants available.
- Manic depression, or bipolar disorder, is diagnosed when periods of mania (hyperactivity, elevated mood, and sometimes irritability) alternate with depression. Sometimes these two mood states occur simultaneously.

WHERE TO START

Do—

- Help teenagers recognize they have a problem.
- Encourage them to make a list of daily self-care activities and practice them.
- Establish communication with others in the teenager's support network.
- Challenge expressions of hopelessness.
- Empathize with their feelings.
- Emphasize that depression is treatable.
- Encourage physical exercise.

Don't—

- Tell a depressed person to "just snap out of it" or "cheer up." Don't expect that they will be able to overcome this without help.

- Use critical or shaming statements.

- Ignore or downplay suicidal thoughts or attempts.

DIGGING DEEPER

Some suggested resources to help you more fully understand kids who are depressed. Use these as starting points if you need to go deeper.

Recommended Reading

Adolescent Depression and Suicide by John S. Wodarski, Ph.D.; Lois A. Wodarski, Ph.D.; and Catherine N. Dulmus, Ph.D.

Adolescents in Crisis: A Guidebook for Parents, Teachers, Ministers, and Counselors by G. Wade Rowatt, Jr.

Help Me, I'm Sad: Recognizing, Treating, and Preventing Childhood and Adolescent Depression by David G. Fassler, M.D. and Lynne S. Dumas.

Surfing the Web

Internet Mental Health: *www.mentalhealth.com*

National Mental Health Association: *www.nmha.org*

Helpguide (for teens): *www.helpguide.org/mental/depression_teen.htm*

Teen Moods (a teen depression support community): *www.teen-moods.net*

Toll-Free Hotlines

Depression and Bipolar Support Alliance (DBSA) Hotline/Support Group: 1-800-826-3632

Covenant House Nineline: 1-800-999-9999

final thoughts

Writing this book hasn't been a lot of fun. Many of the issues we've looked at are heavy and dark. The reality of youth ministry today is that we can't count on one more round of the egg-in-the-armpit relay to address the reality of what's going on in the lives of kids. What kept me going was the hope that you would pick up this book, read it, and be encouraged and equipped in the work you do with kids who are hurting.

A FEW KEY REMINDERS—

Don't underestimate the significance of the relationships you have with the kids who trust you enough to share their hearts with you. One of the biggest risks an adolescent will ever take is to trust an adult with her secrets. We live in different worlds. Although kids desperately need the voice of an adult in their lives, they've seen too many of their friends get hurt in the process. We can't take lightly their willingness to trust us. In our own insecurity, we can easily assume we have little to offer. We may list all kinds of reasons why we aren't qualified to work with wounded kids—too old, untrained, uncool, unresolved issues. But when kids choose to trust us, we have the most significant qualification possible. If we walk away and declare ourselves unfit, they may have no one else to turn to.

Remember: Most kids need a listener first.

Listening takes time and personal discipline. Most of us find it easier to reel off a string of advice and then step back from the relationship, assuming our job is over. Sadly, that's the way most adults, including parents, deal with teenagers. If you can offer a kid a listening heart (not just listening ears), you're giving him a rare gift in his noisy, painful world. More often than not, just the exercise of talking through the issue with someone who truly cares is enough to give a hurting teenager the courage to go another round.

Beware of trivializing kids' pain.

Don't glibly quote Bible verses about everything working out in the end or God wanting to use this to make the kid a better person. Kids are too smart to buy into pat answers and spiritual clichés. They know that people who spout simple steps and formulas to address complex relational issues are usually just covering up their own questions and confusion. Teenagers would rather we genuinely say, "I don't have a clue what to say to you right now" than rattle off a mindless, one-sentence sermon.

Does God want to use this pain to make them better people? Of course he does! Will God work things out for the good of deeply hurting kids? It's in his very nature to do that! I'm not suggesting that biblical truth is of no importance in the life of a hurting teenager. I'm simply reminding us that Scripture is intended as a powerful, penetrating sword—exposing the heart and allowing light to flow into dark places. But when we use it as a cheap bandage to create an illusion of healing, it loses all its clout.

Refer kids if you need to—but DO NOT back away from them.

Just because kids may have "professionals" working with them now doesn't mean they don't still need you. We've talked about the importance of recognizing your limits and inviting someone else to help when you get out of your depth. It's the loving thing to do to make sure the kids you care about are getting the best possible help. Don't forget that what you have to offer them is still very important. A kid shares her heart with you because she trusts and respects you. The person you referred her to may have legitimate expertise—and that will be crucial to a happy ending—but remember that your friendship is precious to her, and what the adolescent needs from you is your heart, not your head.

You are not in this alone!

The job of caring for a hurting kid is bigger than even the most qualified among us are equipped to handle. Don't forget—Jesus is the Wonderful Counselor. He invites us to partner with him as willing apprentices, giving healing and hope to the kids he loves. The work we do with hurting students is important—but we're not alone. May God find us faithful in this amazing task he's given to us—all of us.